THE MINISTER'S MARRIAGE HANDBOOK

THE MINISTER'S
MARRIAGE
HANDBOOK

BY JAMES L. CHRISTENSEN

FLEMING H. REVELL COMPANY
OLD TAPPAN • NEW JERSEY

Permission to quote the following material was given by the respective publishers.

The "Checklist for Bride and Groom" (p. 22) is from *Your Wedding Workbook*, by Natalia Beiting and James R. Hine (Danville, Ill., Interstate Printers and Publishers, Inc., 1963, pp. 3, 4).

The listing of wedding music (p. 35) is published with permission of The West Side Presbyterian Church of Ridgewood, N.J.

Counseling procedures (pp. 55–6) by George C. Desmond are from his article, "A Program of Premarital Counseling," which appeared in *Pulpit Digest* (Oct., 1963, pp. 17–21).

Procedures by Oliver M. Butterfield are from *Premarital Counseling: A Manual of Suggestions for Ministers*. Published by the Federal Council of Churches of Christ in America. Copyright 1945.

Counseling procedures (pp. 57–8), "Details of Wedding Form" (pp. 31, 32), and "Clergyman's Marriage Information and Permanent Record" (pp. 61–3) are from *Grounds for Marriage*, by James R. Hine (Danville, Ill., Interstate Printers and Publishers, Inc., 1962, pp. vii, viii, 75–7).

The "State Laws of Divorce" chart (pp. 112–14) is reprinted from *The 1966 World Almanac and Book of Facts*, New York.

The wedding prayer by C. Neil Strait (pp. 117–18) is from the June, 1964, issue of *Pulpit Digest*, p. 46.

The newlyweds' prayer by Percy Roy Hayward (p. 119) is from his book, *Young People's Prayers* (New York, Association Press, 1945, p. 62).

The wedding benediction by Roy A. Burkhart (p. 120) is from his book, *Secret of a Happy Marriage* (New York, Harper & Row Publishers, Inc., 1949, p. 63).

The Baptist marriage service (pp. 120–4) is from *The Pastor's Manual* by James Randolph Hobbs (Nashville, Tenn., Broadman Press, 1955, pp. 151–6).

A Disciple's marriage service (pp. 124–9) is reprinted from *Christian Worship—A Service Book*, edited by G. Edwin Osborn (St. Louis, Mo., The Bethany Press, 1953, pp. 67–72).

The Community or Congregational service (pp. 130–2) is from *Secret of a Happy Marriage*, by Roy A. Burkhart (New York, Harper & Row Publishers, Inc., 1949, pp. 60–3).

The Presbyterian service (pp. 133–6) is from *The Book of Common Worship*, 1946. The Presbyterian Board of Christian Education.

The Methodist service (pp. 136–40) is from *Ritual, The Methodist Church*. Copyright © 1964, Board of Publication of The Methodist Church, Inc.

The Lutheran service (pp. 140–5) is reprinted from *The Pastor's Companion* (St. Louis, Mo., Concordia Publishing House, pp. 35–41).

The Episcopal service (pp. 145–9) is from *The Book of Common Prayer* of the Episcopal Church.

The general marriage service (pp. 149–51) is from *Manual of Forms for Ministers*, by Benjamin L. Smith (St. Louis, Christian Board of Publication, 1919, pp. 17–19).

The order of blessing of a civil marriage (pp. 151–3) is adapted from *Devotional Services for Public Worship*, by John Hunter (New York, E. P. Dutton & Co., Inc., and London, J. M. Dent & Sons Ltd.).

To our two teen-age daughters, Lynda and Becky, who have filled our home with joy, and for whom we pray a happy Christian marriage.

Preface

A wedding held in a church should be a Christian service of worship.

However, as George Hedley has written, "Nothing associated with the Church has been allowed to become so trivial, so irreligious, so much a display and so little a solemnization, as has the typical society wedding of our time. And the economically underprivileged, aping those who scarcely are their betters, have fallen into their own rather pathetic variations of the same bad taste and the same total lack of religious meaning."[1]

Persons planning weddings are inclined to consider what is pretty, glamorous, and impressive, rather than what is consistent and appropriate for a church marriage service. Too frequently, florists, decorators, and Emily Post have been consulted for information about what is proper, when the church's minister should be the one to interpret the significance of marriage in a church.

Christian marriage is not *just* matrimony; it is *holy* matrimony. It is not an estate instituted by man; it is an estate instituted by God. Church is the proper place to celebrate Christian marriage; and the minister, as God's representative, is the key person in making more consistent and orderly the wedding service to the glory of God.

It is with the above conviction that this handbook has been prepared. At the outset, the author recognized the divergent viewpoints and practices of ministers, churches, and laymen. It is hoped, however, that the present material is sufficiently flexible, general, and nondogmatic as to be helpful, at least in part, to ministers of all persuasions.

JAMES L. CHRISTENSEN

Enid, Oklahoma

Contents

                            9

I. The Spiritual Significance of the Wedding Service

What is the significance of being married in a church? To be sure, a church wedding is not a show or an entertainment. It is a service to Almighty God.

The minister begins the wedding service with such words as: "Dearly beloved, we are gathered together here in the presence of God to join this man and this woman in holy matrimony, an estate instituted by God, regulated by His commandments, and to be held in honor among all men." The first fact of Christian marriage is that it is undertaken in the presence of God. It is holy matrimony, instituted *by God,* not by man. By marrying in a church, the bride and groom affirm that God joins them together. Central attention is not focused on the bride, but on God, the One "altogether lovely." Hence, marriage "is not to be entered into unadvisably or lightly, but reverently, discreetly, soberly, and in the fear of God." In Christian marriage, it is God who matters most of all. The relationship is to be regulated by His commandments.

Most ceremonies include such words as: "Marriage is to be held in honor among all men," or "If any of you know cause, or just impediment, why these two persons should not be joined in holy matrimony, you are to declare it." One of the main features of the wedding service in the Judaic and Christian tradition is its public character.[1] Though marriage is intensely personal and intimate, it is never a completely private matter. Society is involved "for better or for worse"; family traditions and reputations are implicated. "Who giveth this woman to be joined to this man?"—When the father has identified himself and gives the family's public approval, and the daughter withdraws

13

her hand, the way is open for the new relationship to be established. Marriage is a highly pleasurable undertaking, but it is not primarily a device designed to provide personal pleasures for two people.

The union is likely to produce children, who may be either a burden or a strength to the community. Hence, each marriage is of concern to all. The "family" is a fundamental unit of society, for it is the medium to propagate the human race, to satisfy emotional needs in beneficial ways, and to perpetuate religious experience. The community has a stake in every new union. The "secret" marriage is a contradiction in terms, and a "quickie" marriage indicates failure to appreciate this public character. This public significance of marriage has led to the establishment of laws whereby the marriage intention is acknowledged openly prior to the solemnizing of it.

The religious wedding service, in essence, is the giving of public approval to the union by the family, the church, and the community. Marriage, therefore, is not to be entered into lightly, but "reverently, discreetly, and soberly," and in the presence of those whose approbation and blessing the couple seek.

Furthermore, the religious wedding service is the recognition before God that marriage is a lifelong commitment. It is not a mere contract or bargain which has certain contingencies and escape clauses. The two participants in marriage pledge themselves "for better, for worse; for richer, for poorer; in sickness and in health." It frankly recognizes in advance the possibilities of economic difficulties, illness, sterility, and other dangers and pitfalls. Nonetheless, marriage is not conceived as a temporary arrangement, to be honored only so long as relationships are mutually pleasant; rather, it is a pledge to be respected "so long as we both shall live."

Hence, it is intrinsically a relationship of mutually corresponding obligations. The ceremony includes such thoughts as: "Our Lord through his apostles has instructed those who enter this relation to cherish a mutual esteem and love; to bear with each other's infirmities and weaknesses; to comfort each other in sickness, trouble, and sorrow; in honesty and industry to provide for each other and for their household in temporal things; to pray for and encourage each other in the things that pertain to God; and to live together as heirs of his grace." When a minister says to the man and woman before him, "I therefore require and charge you both," he does not use empty phrases.

Marriage is an arrangement in which each partner gives *all* that he has: "with all my worldly goods I thee endow." A marriage is not a marriage at all if it is partial or entered into with fingers crossed or with the idea that it is but a temporary trial that can be dissolved at the divorce court if unsatisfactory. There must be a mutual outpouring of unlimited love. A truly married person is more interested in his mate's happiness than in his own. The wedding is the sacred service during which a man and a woman make these vows of lifelong fidelity.

Since marriage is a venture of faith, the wedding ceremony is, in reality, the couple's acceptance of the church's faith.[2] The couple speak for themselves while they stand at the foot of the chancel steps. The minister asks the groom, and then the bride: "Will you love, comfort, honor, and keep (him or her) in sickness and in health; and forsaking all others, keep yourself only unto (him or her) so long as you both shall live?" Each responds, "I will." Thus, the gulf is spanned between the faith of the church and the faith of the persons who come to the church to be married. The attitude of the church toward marriage is that it is a holy relationship. It is a life of loving, comforting, honoring, and keeping; there is no wavering in sickness or in health; and, from the day of marriage to the day of death, no other man or woman shall invade the sacred precincts of sexual union. For nineteen centuries this has also been the faith of the church. With the speaking of the words "I will," the faith of the church is accepted by the couple; this is the kind of relationship they intend their marriage to be.

The man and the woman ascend the chancel steps to the altar to make their promises to one another. Looking into each other's eyes, they repeat the words which bind their lives together for the rest of their days on earth: "I, John, take thee, Mary, to be my wedded wife, to have and to hold, from this day forward . . . till death do us part." To bring to remembrance the wedding day and to seal the promises, ring symbols are exchanged, "in token and pledge of constant faith and abiding love." The wedding ceremony is the public acceptance of the bond which limits free expression. The possibility of dating or making love with others is ruled out by virtue of the wedding bond. The pledge of fidelity and the dedication to faithfulness are implied in the ring exchange. Marriage is not compatible with absolute freedom, yet the person who binds himself to one life-mate finds the highest level of freedom.

The sacredness of the wedding ring was understood by Carl Sandburg's mother. Said he, "Mama's wedding ring was never lost—was always on that finger, placed there with pledges years ago. It was a sign and seal of something that ran deep and held fast between the two of them. They had chosen each other as partners. . . ." So should it be for all who are joined in holy matrimony.

Speaking as an agent of the living God and as a representative of the whole community, the minister pronounces that the union is indeed a fact: "I pronounce that they are husband and wife. . . . What God, then, has joined together, let no man put asunder."

The basis of unity is the fact that in this bond two persons are joined together so as to become "one flesh." ". . . they are no longer two individuals: they are one flesh" (MATTHEW 19:6, *NEB*).

This unity of two in one flesh is not just biological, as it is for animals; rather, it also has spiritual and psychic qualities. Marriage brings into play, not just two biological beings, but two personalities. The dialogue is of the spirit; the kiss is of the soul; the spirit's intensity is echoed by the flesh.

Nowhere in Scripture is marriage discussed in terms of sex; instead, it is discussed in terms of knowledge. The closest union that exists between anything in the universe and man himself is possible only through knowledge. When man knows a flower or a tree, he "possesses" these objects within his mind.

Similarly, marriage involves the mind, soul, heart, and will, as well as the reproductive organs. It is one of the closest unions possible, more personal than carnal. The union is something more than the physical union of the two sexes; the union is psychosomatic, affecting the whole person, body and soul. In the moment of "knowing," each partner receives a gift which neither ever knew before. Henceforth, the woman can never return to her virginity; the man can never return to ignorance. Something happens in oneness; and from that oneness comes fidelity.

The ceremony ends, and a great new life begins, hallowed in the spirit of prayer: "The Lord bless, preserve, and keep you; the Lord mercifully with his favor look upon you, and fill you with all spiritual benediction and grace; that you may so live together in this life that in the world to come you may have life everlasting."

TRADITIONAL CHURCH WEDDING SERVICE

For the greatest spiritual significance, the wedding ceremony should be set in a worship framework, with appropriate music content. The traditional and generally accepted wedding service plan used in most churches is as follows:

> *Prelude music*
> *Seating of guests*
> *Lighting of candles*
> *Groom's parents seated*
> *Bride's mother seated*

Aisle cloth unrolled
Vocal music
The wedding processional
The marriage ceremony
The wedding recessional
Bride's parents ushered out
Groom's parents ushered out
Congregation dismissed

Slight alterations are often made in this procedure, in accordance with local policy, practice, or desire.

WEDDING WORSHIP SERVICE

Some churches follow a form for the wedding not unlike the traditional order for Sunday morning worship. There is much to commend this increasingly used plan, because the wedding service is not entertainment and it is not a theatrical show—it is worship. Primary attention should not be focused on the bride, however beautiful she may be—rather, on God. The following order is recommended as truest to the best worship content. (A bulletin, much like the guide for a formal morning worship service, is presented to those attending.)

Prelude: J. S. Bach, "In Thee Is Gladness"; Marcello, "Psalm 19"; Stamitz, "Andante"
Lighting of Candles
Opening sentences: A call by the minister for worship to begin.
Processional hymn: "Love Divine, All Love Excelling" (sung by the whole congregation, standing)
Statement to congregation: "We are gathered to perform a ceremony of holy matrimony."
Prayer of confession: "We acknowledge our status before God."
Words of assurance: The minister proclaims the good news that God does indeed forgive us.
Old Testament lesson: Ruth 1:16

Solo or anthem: "O Perfect Love"
New Testament lesson: I Corinthians 13:4-7
Witness to the word: The minister, in a brief witness, may speak of the significance of marriage in the Christian tradition.
Exchanging of vows
Recessional hymn
(sung by the whole congregation, standing)
Benediction
Postlude

During the singing of the processional hymn, the wedding party proceeds down the aisle to the front pew. The bride's party is seated on the right side; the groom's party on the left side. The minister takes his place behind the pulpit. The service proceeds as outlined. At the time for the exchanging of vows, the party rises and comes forward to the chancel, where the minister meets them. The service proceeds in a manner similar to a regular worship service. Procedures of the ceremony are similar to those described in chapter IX. The ceremonies included in this volume can be adapted to the above service plan.

II. The Details of Wedding Planning

THE OFFICIATING MINISTER

People should be married by their own minister, if at all possible, in order that there may be a permanent relationship between the officiating minister and the family which he helps to bring into existence. When young people are married by an outsider, the occasion is robbed of some of the intimate values.

It is a matter of ministerial ethics that a minister does not return to a former parish to perform pastoral duties or assume privileges. The rare occasion for acceptance of such participation may be on the condition that he is invited by the local minister to assist. It is quite easy for a minister to say to a family or a prospective bride who asks him to officiate in his former parish: "I am sorry. As much as I would like to participate, I cannot presume upon the privilege of the local minister. With his invitation, I might assist him in the service. You talk with him about it."

Often the church policy can strengthen this position and save the church's minister from much embarrassment by stating that "a staff member of the local church must be a part of all weddings held." Thus, the outside minister would have an assisting role only.

PLACE OF THE WEDDING

Young people should be married in their own communities, so that parents, relatives, and friends may attend. If they come from different communities, the wedding is usually held in the bride's community. A marriage is of concern to all who are close to those who marry; the ceremony is made public because, in essence, it implies community approval.

Stunt weddings, or obscure, sensational locations for weddings, are to be discouraged, because such rob marriage of the intimate and sacred values.

It is strongly recommended that persons be married in the sanctuary or chapel of the church. The atmosphere would be one that lends reverence and a spirit of worship, thus contributing to the essential nature of marriage.

DUTIES OF THE BRIDE AND HER FAMILY

The date, place, and time of the ceremony are selected by the bride and her mother. They also schedule the church and the pastor, obtain an organist and a singer, and arrange for the rehearsal of the wedding party at the church. The bride and her mother select the invitations, make up the guest list (after conferring with the groom's mother), and send out invitations. The selection of the style and color of the bridesmaids' dresses is up to the bride; however, she does not pay for them. Decorations and flowers for the church, the ring for the future husband, and the wedding reception are responsibilities of the bride's family. The bride also has the social obligation of acknowledging receipt of each wedding gift with a personal note.

DUTIES OF THE GROOM

The groom purchases the marriage license, the ring, bouquet, and wedding gift for his bride, as well as the ties, boutonnieres, or other gifts, as regional customs demand, for the men of the wedding party. Also, he arranges the rehearsal dinner. One of his most important duties is to make advance arrangements for the honeymoon trip, so that accommodations are assured.

FINANCIAL OBLIGATIONS OF THE BRIDE

Since the major portion of the wedding expenses falls on the bride's family, there has been justifiable agitation in some churches against elaborate ceremonies, flowers, receptions, and the like. It seems more rational to use money that could be squandered on "extras" for more enduring and essential purchases. The sensible girl does not insist that her family go into near-bankruptcy in order that she have an elaborate wedding. The minister can urge simplicity in decorations, dress, and accompanying arrangements. The bride's financial responsibilities are as follows:

Engraving of invitations and announcements
Mailing of invitations, cards, and announcements
Transportation for attendants to and from church
Hotel bills for her attendants when bride's parents cannot accomodate them
Organist
Soloist
Rental of church and custodial fees
Wedding reception

Groom's ring
Bride's trousseau
Wedding photographs
Gifts to the bridesmaids and maid (or matron) of honor
Bridesmaids' flowers
Church decorations
Gift to groom

FINANCIAL OBLIGATIONS OF THE GROOM

Marriage license
Bride's ring
Bachelor dinner (optional)
Rehearsal dinner
Gift to bride
Bride's flowers
Transportation for male attendants to and from church
Clergyman's fee
Corsages for the mothers of the bride and the groom
Boutonnieres for best man, ushers, groomsmen, groom's
father, and the minister
Gifts to male attendants and ushers
Ties and gloves for attendants (optional)
Hotel bills for his attendants from out of town
Wedding trip

CHECKLIST FOR BRIDE AND GROOM[1]

The following list could be mimeographed and given to the bride at the first conference:

Twelfth Week Before Wedding

1. Have conference with minister to arrange day and time.
2. Make reservation for church use for both wedding and reception. If reception is not in a church, you may have to make earlier arrangements.
3. Learn the policy of the church regarding costs, decorations, etc.
4. Schedule at least one or two more premarital counseling sessions.
5. Make arrangements with organist, other musicians, and primary attendants.
6. Read through a wedding planning book.

Eleventh Week Before Wedding
1. Make out wedding invitation list.
2. Make out reception list.
3. Make out announcement list.
4. Order invitations and announcements.
5. Have conference with the caterer.

Tenth Week Before Wedding
1. Select and get commitments from members of the wedding party.
2. Choose general color scheme and flowers.

Ninth and Eighth Weeks Before Wedding
1. Order or begin making wedding dress.
2. Arrange date, time, and place of rehearsal dinner.
3. Select china, glassware, and silver patterns.

Seventh Week Before Wedding
1. Make arrangements with florist.
2. Make arrangements with photographer.
3. Order printed napkins, etc., for reception.
4. Have conference with minister.

Sixth Week Before Wedding
1. Pick out gifts for attendants.
2. Arrange for housing of guests from out of town.
3. Read literature recommended by the minister.
4. Buy wedding rings.

Fifth Week Before the Wedding
1. Buy going-away clothes.
2. Make honeymoon trip reservations.

Fourth Week Before Wedding
1. Have conference with physician.
2. Have blood test.
3. Recheck with all attendants to confirm that they will be present.
4. Send out invitations to wedding and to rehearsal dinner.
5. Submit a release to newspaper of announced wedding plans.

Third Week Before Wedding
1. Give a bridesmaids' luncheon or tea.

Second Week Before Wedding
1. Get license.
2. Have conference with minister.
3. Pose a bride's picture for newspaper.

Last Week Before Wedding
1. Remind all participants regarding rehearsal attendance.
2. Have newspaper release ready.
3. Arrange for announcements to be mailed the day of the ceremony.

FLORAL DECORATIONS

A wedding is a time for simplicity and good taste, with particular moderation advisable in the selection of floral displays. There is no need for extreme decoration in the sanctuary; the use of arches, bells, trees, too many flowers, and candles, are common abuses. One gets the impression at times that some families attempt to outdo other families with ornament and display.

One well-known church allows the display of only one large bouquet for all weddings, however large or small. This rule prevents indulgence in competition and the desire to impress others.

Of course, the wish for a wedding of aesthetic beauty is normal, natural, and desirable. However, gaudiness and extremes should be avoided.

The basic principle is this: the simpler the decorations, the better. Decorations should neither distract from nor obscure the chancel furniture, the symbolism of the sanctuary, or the wedding service. The sanctuary itself should reflect in symbols and beauty the love of God and the spirit of Christ.

The minister should inform local florists of the rules of his church with regard to wedding decorations, plus his own personal preferences regarding same. Implicit understanding is needed with florists regarding the moving of chancel furniture, the places where flowers are to be located, and the use of tape and tacks.

DUTIES OF THE MAID (OR MATRON) OF HONOR

The maid of honor is the bride's most important attendant, usually being her sister or closest friend. She should be notified of her selection several months in advance, before invitations are sent, so that the date can be entered into her schedule and necessary adjustments and clothing preparations can be made.

Unless the bride can afford the expense and wants to give her the wedding outfit, the maid of honor buys her own wedding clothes. The flowers which she carries, however, are given to her by the bride.

The duties and responsibilities of the maid of honor are as follows:

1. Attend the rehearsal.
2. Arrange the bride's train as the procession forms in the rear of the church, and again at the altar if necessary, and straighten it behind the bride as she turns for the recessional.
3. Hold the bride's bouquet during the ring-exchange.
4. Carry the groom's ring during the ceremony (unless there is a ring-bearer), and give it to the minister at the appropriate time.
5. If the bride wears a veil, the maid of honor helps to lift it back on her head at the end of the ceremony.
6. Stand in the receiving line next to the groom.
7. Assist the bride in changing clothes and packing for her trip.
8. See that no tricks in bad taste are played.

DUTIES OF THE BEST MAN

The best man is the groom's primary attendant, and is usually his closest friend or a brother. He is chosen in ample time so that he can make whatever adjustments are necessary to be present.

Among the duties of the best man are:

1. Aid the groom in every possible way in preparation for the wedding. He protects the groom from pranks, and

under no circumstance participates in practical jokes played on the bride and groom.

2. Attend the rehearsal; and aid the minister in gaining the cooperation of the male attendants and seeing that they are on time for the wedding.

3. Help the groom dress for the wedding, and go with him to the church at least a half hour before wedding time.

4. Deliver the license and wedding book to the minister for his recording, sign his own signature as one of the witnesses, and deliver the same to the maid of honor for her signature.

5. Give the clergyman his fee, inconspicuously, in a plain, white, sealed envelope.

6. Accompany the groom to the altar, carrying the bride's ring until the time the minister asks for it in the ceremony. If the groom wears gloves, the best man holds them during the ceremony.

7. Stand in the reception line next to the maid of honor. If the reception is at a place other than the church, he gets the hats and coats of the bride and groom and meets them at the front door. He chauffeurs the couple and maid of honor to the place of the reception.

8. Help the groom pack, and take charge of the couple's luggage, seeing that it is placed safely in the going-away car.

9. Keep in safety the keys to the groom's car. When the time comes for the couple's departure, he helps them get away safely.

THE CHURCH'S WEDDING POLICY

Each congregation should have a carefully prepared, official policy regarding wedding arrangements. This is essential for directing the ministerial staff, the business and custodial personnel, and the bridal family. There are, of course, scores of churches which have been the scenes of many weddings for years upon years, with no definite policies. Arrangements have been at the discretion of the pastor, policies changing with succeeding pastors. Other churches have had unwritten policies known generally by the membership. Others have adopted new plans for each individual marriage.

However, in order to avoid misunderstandings and to make the planning parties aware of the responsibilities involved, it seems best to have a definite policy.

This may already be determined by the specific denomination. In most cases, the local, legislative, policy-making body (such as the trustees, general board, or session) initiates such directives. For most effective use, the policy should be printed and made available to the bride at the initial conference about the wedding. Publication of the policy in the church newspaper is important, to inform the congregation.

The policy should cover such matters as: the church facilities available and the cost for members and non-members, the services the church staff renders, the reception possibilities, acceptable music, the number of pre-marital conferences expected, and rules regarding decorations, photographs, the use of rice and confetti, smoking, and consumption of alcoholic beverages.

The basic purpose of such a policy should not be to discourage church weddings. To the contrary, the church wishes to encourage its people to have sacred wedding services in the church. Hence, the policy should be sufficiently flexible to allow variations of taste and sufficiently modest so that none are discouraged financially. Usually, it is wise to give the pastor the authority to alter financial obligations if and when there is sufficient need in his judgment.

SAMPLE CHURCH POLICY[2]

Presented here is a sample policy which one church has adopted. It may not be appropriate to follow where there is a large, multiple staff, and costs may vary for different churches.

"Central Christian Church wants to render the best possible service to its members and friends. You are welcome to the use of our facilities.

"The wedding ceremony is one of the most sacred rites of the church. It is the desire of the pastor and the church family to make every such ceremony a beautiful and worshipful experience. We extend to each wedding party every possible courtesy and assistance.

"To make available our services, the following procedures have been adopted.

Minister

"The minister shall officiate at all marriages in the church, except in unusual situations where other arrangements are made with the pastor. In the absence of the minister, another ordained staff member will be assigned.

"Ministers of other denominations shall be free to use the facilities and perform the ceremony according to the rites of their respective church, subject to the approval of the pastor of this church.

"The bride and groom shall arrange a premarital conference with the minister as far in advance of the ceremony as possible. This conference should be held before the announcements are made or invitations printed. The minister will provide literature and advice which will be helpful for properly preparing for marriage.

"The pastor will conduct the rehearsal with the assistance of the cateress, if desired, on the evening before the wedding.

"No specific charge is made for the minister's services except as in keeping with the usual custom. Such arrangement is private and not the church's responsibility.

Music

"Music used with the ceremony should be in keeping with the sacredness and dignity of the wedding service.

"When the organ is desired, the church organist is to be used unless another request is made through the minister who will also recommend a soloist if requested. Fees for the soloist and organist are a private arrangement and should be so arranged in advance.

Photographs

"Photographs may not be taken during the ceremony proper. Pictures may be taken during the processional and recessional. After the recessional, the wedding party may return for as many pictures as are desired.

Floral Decorations

"Florists are required to clear with the church receptionist prior to decorating the church, or any portion thereof.

"Flowers used must be in clean, rust-free, leak-proof containers.

"Only dripless candles may be used to prevent drippings on the floor; a protective covering under the candelabra is required. In the event of dripping on furniture, floor, or carpets, the florist shall be responsible for cleaning and reimbursement for damage.

"Church premises shall be left as clean as possible after removal of decorations.

Rice and Confetti

"Rice and confetti throwing is to be done outside the building, not on the inside.

Receptions

"Receptions held in church building must be under the direction of staff cateress, unless other arrangements are made with the pastor.

"The church's punch bowl, silver service, cups, silverware, and linens are available, if desired.

Use of Alcoholic Beverages

"It is expected that members of the wedding party will refrain from alcoholic beverages immediately preceding both the rehearsal and the wedding. No alcoholic beverages are to be used in the punch. There shall be no smoking in the sanctuary, or reception room. The bride and groom shall make these rules known to all members of the wedding party.

Fees

FOR CEREMONY:

Area	Seating	Members	Nonmembers
Sanctuary with air-conditioning or heat if necessary for both rehearsal and wedding	400	$25	$40
Chapel	175	$15	$30
Parsonage air-conditioning	15	no cost	no cost

FOR RECEPTION:

Area	Seating	
Social Hall	400	A deposit of $35 shall be made which will include: cateress fee, custodian fee, rental of chinaware and dishwashing. Cost of cake and punch ingredients will be billed to the bride's family.
Loggia	200	
Parlor	50	

"Fees shall be paid to receptionist or financial secretary when reservations are made or in advance of wedding. Exceptions to these fees may be made by the minister where in his opinion the payment would be a hardship and might deprive the couple of a church wedding.

"In case there is a need to request arrangements differing from those outlined, such requests should be made to the minister before the rehearsal and/or wedding. The cateress and custodian do not have authority to make changes from these policies."

CLERGYMAN'S FEE:

Today's salary schedules for ministers in most denominations make it unnecessary for the clergyman to depend upon wedding fees for his expenses. Ideally, he should perform all of his ministerial duties as a part of his vocation, and be paid an adequate salary by the congregation, without dependence upon gratuities. Freedom from such dependence helps the minister to refuse the temptation to marry eloping lovers and those whom, in good conscience, he prefers not to marry.

However, it is a tradition that the minister be given a modest, monetary gift as an expression of appreciation. This is a legitimate practice, and such a gift can be accepted without apology because the conscientious minister spends many hours in the preparation for and performing of a wedding. Because of the service rendered in a wedding ceremony and the amount of time consumed, if anyone deserves a gratuity, it is undoubtedly the minister. However, it is most unbecoming and inappropriate for a Christian minister to "have his hand out" for a tip, to give the impression in any way that he expects a fee, or to establish a definite charge for his services.

DETAILS OF WEDDING FORM[3]

Wedding of:

_____

_____

1. Date of ceremony_____ Time_____
   Formal_____ Semiformal_____ Informal_____
2. Place ceremony will be held_____
   Estimate of attendance_____
3. Date of wedding rehearsal_____ Time_____
4. Will all be present for rehearsal?_____
   Will there be a rehearsal dinner?_____.

5. Single ring_____Double ring_____
   Will bride be given away?_____
6. Will there be music?____ Organist?____ Soloist?____
7. Will there be a reception? _____
8. Plans for decorations_____
9. Plans for photographs (check church regulations)____
   _____

10. Bride's attendants:
    Maid (or matron) of honor_____
    Bridesmaids_____
    Flower girl and/or ring-bearer_____
11. Groom's attendants:
    Best man_____
    Groomsmen_____
    Ushers_____

Schedule of interviews with clergyman or counselor:

	Date	Time
1.	_____	_____
2.	_____	_____
3.	_____	_____

Date of interview with staff member in charge of arrangements for church and reception rooms_____

III. Wedding Music

Because music is usually an integral part of the marriage service, the minister cannot be indifferent to the type of music used, nor can he totally abdicate making decisions regarding such to the whim or fancy of the bride. The bride may be totally unaware of what is fitting music for a religious service, or too inexperienced musically to have good judgment regarding appropriate selections. Too much music is chosen on the basis of its being the romantic, secular selections which were the couple's favorites during their courtship. Other couples choose popular, Broadway show music they consider entertaining. The minister might suggest that these selections be sung either at the rehearsal dinner or at the reception following the wedding, if the bride is insistent that they be used.

The minister has a responsibility to give early directives for the selection of music which will help maintain the dignity, meaning, and spiritual basis of the marriage service. Wedding music should be "God-centered," rather than "bride-centered." Each minister should tactfully direct this area according to his church's policy, without injuring the feelings of the persons involved. The minister may submit a listing of what his church considers appropriate or acceptable music from which the bride and groom may choose. Some ministers are rigidly strict; others prefer to indicate the ideal music but retain some flexibility. I have always believed it better to sacrifice quality occasionally, if rigidity jeopardizes a good relationship with those who have predetermined selections and have no disposition to change them.

The much-used, traditional Wagner and Mendelssohn wedding marches are being omitted from marriage services in many churches, and replaced by great processional hymns. The reasons have much merit.[1] The "Here Comes the Bride" chorus from Wagner's *Lohengrin* was never intended for church use. In the opera, this excerpt occurs when the bride and groom enter the bridal chamber, and the bed is being readied. The music is even more incongruous for use at a wedding when one considers that, before the act is over, the bridegroom has murdered a rival and is forced to abandon his wife forever. The Mendelssohn music was composed as an accompaniment to

Shakespeare's *A Midsummer Night's Dream*. A musical fantasy, attention is centered on a workman named Bottom, who is transformed into a jackal. The jackal courts and bewitches a fairy. The play is filled with sensuality and magic, and is inappropriate for a Christian wedding.

It takes a diplomatic, courageous, and persuasive minister to break with the popular practices that have infiltrated the church, and to win the cooperation of his church leadership and membership, and of the wedding parties in particular. If possible, however, he should begin somehow, somewhere, to raise the standards and choose music which is consistent with the church's worship.

Excellent and appropriate *prelude* music includes: Bach's "In Thee Is Gladness," Marcello's "Psalm Nineteen," Benoit's "Fifty Elevations," and Stamitz's "Andante." Hymns about the family are appropriate.

Acceptable *processional* or *recessional* hymns are: "Love Divine," "We Gather Together," "Praise the Lord, Ye Heavens, Adore Him," "Now Thank We All Our God," "Praise to the Lord, the Almighty," "All Glory, Laud and Honor," "Glorious Things of Thee Are Spoken."

Some ministers prefer only organ music for the wedding. The organist who plays at the wedding should be the regular church organist or assistant organist, since they are familiar with the church's instrument and their ability is known and accepted by the minister. If the bride desires a friend to play the organ, approval should be obtained from the music committee, the minister, or the church organist.

When vocal music is desired, it may be by the choir, an ensemble, or a soloist. When it is desired that there be a vocal soloist, it is wise for the minister to recommend a singer from among the church singers, rather than to have a friend of the bride sing, who may or may not have the ability or the proper repertoire to make the spiritual contribution. If the bride desires a particular person to sing, it might be suggested that the singer audition with the organist for approval a month prior to the wedding.

LISTINGS OF APPROPRIATE WEDDING MUSIC

PRESBYTERIAN LIST

A minister of The West Side Presbyterian Church, Ridgewood, N.J., submits the following list to the bride at the initial planning conference, with attached notation:

"This is a partial list, on which planning can begin. The Minister of Music will be happy to play any of the below listed music by appointment, to help you in your selection."

ORGAN MUSIC
Bach—My Spirit, Be Joyful!
    Our Father Which Art in Heaven
    My Heart Ever Faithful (ed., Gigout)
    Jesus, Joy of Man's Desiring
    Sheep May Safely Graze
    Deck Thyself, My Soul, with Gladness
    Sleepers, Wake!
    In Thee Is Gladness
    Rejoice, Beloved Christians
    If Thou Art Near
    St. Ann Fugue
    Allegro (Concerto in A Minor, after Vivaldi)
    Air in D (also other Airs, Adagios)
    Siciliano in C Minor
    Sinfonia to Cantata 142*
    From Heaven Above (2 settings)*
    Now Thank We All Our God (ed., Fox)
    In Dulci Jubilo*
Boellmann—Gothic Suite (Chorale and Prayer)
Brahms—A Lovely Rose Is Blooming*
    My Faithful Heart Rejoices
Buxtehude—Fugue in C
Corelli—Adagio in B Minor

    * Especially good in December.

Franck—Chorales (three)
    Adagio (Fantasie in C)
    Prelude, Fugue and Variation
Frescobaldi—Toccata per l'Elevazione
Handel—Water Music (Allegro, Air, Allegro Maestoso)
    Fireworks Music (Overture, The Rejoicing, The
        Peace, Finale)
    The Faithful Shepherd
    Pastorale Symphony (Messiah)*
Karg-Elert—O God, Thou Faithful God
Manz—"Hyfrydol" and other chorale improvizations
Marcello—Psalm 18
    Psalm 20
Mendelssohn—Adagio (Sonata I)
    Allegro Maestoso (Sonata II)
Peeters—Aria, Op. 51
Purcell—Trumpet Tune and Air
    Trumpet Voluntary
Purvis—Canzona on "Leibster Jesu"
    Pastorale on "Forest Green"
    Communion
Vaughan Williams—Prelude on "Rhosymedre"
Wetzler—Processional on "Westminster Abbey"
Widor—Andante Cantabile (Organ Symphony IV)
Wright—Brother James' Air

VOCAL MUSIC
Bach—My Heart Ever Faithful
    Jesus, Joy of Man's Desiring
    God My Shepherd Walks Beside Me
Barnby—O Perfect Love
Bitgood—Though I Speak with the Tongue of Men and of
        Angels
Bunjes—Love Divine
Buxtehude—My Jesus Is My Lasting Joy (altered)
Dvorak—I Will Sing New Songs of Gladness
Franck—O Lord Most Holy (Panis Angelicus)

Handel—Thanks Be to Thee
Jacob—Brother James' Air (Psalm 23)
Mendelssohn—If with All Your Hearts
Mozart—Alleluia!
Williams—A Wedding Prayer

PROCESSIONALS
Bach—Air in D
Haydn-Brahms—Chorale, "St. Antoni"
Purcell—Trumpet Voluntary

Hymn-tunes
Goss—Praise My Soul the King of Heaven
Handel—Thine Is the Glory
Beethoven—Hymn to Joy

RECESSIONALS AND POSTLUDES
Campra—Rigaudon
Coke-Jephcott—Bishop's Promenade
Karg-Elert—Now Thank We All Our God
Marcello—Psalm 20
Mendelssohn—Wedding March
Mulet—Carillon-Sortie
Widor—Toccata (Organ Symphony V)

FANFARES
Bax—For the Wedding of Elisabeth II
Purcell—Fanfare in C

GENERAL LIST

PRELUDES
Bach—Jesus, Joy of Man's Desiring
    In Dulci Jubilo
Bairstow—Evening Song
Batiste—Offertoire
Boellmann—Suite Gothique

Brahms—A Lovely Rose is Blooming
Guilmant—Movements from Sonatas (selected)
James—Meditation à Ste. Clothilde
Karg-Elert—Claire De Lune
Massenet—The Angelus
McKinley—Cantilene
Mendelssohn—Movements from Sonatas (selected)
Rheinberger—Movements from Sonatas (selected)
Wely—Andante in F

Vocal Solos

Barnby—O Perfect Love
Beethoven—I Love Thee
Burleigh—O Perfect Love
Clokey—Set Me as a Seal
Diggle—A Wedding Prayer
Gorton—Entreat Me Not to Leave Thee
Malotte—The Lord's Prayer
Mendelssohn—If With All Your Hearts
Root—Love Never Faileth

Anthems for Choir or Ensemble

Bach—Now Thank We All Our God
Franck—O Lord Most Holy
Handel—Thanks Be to Thee
　　　　The King of Love My Shepherd Is
Stainer—God So Loved the World

Processional or Recessional

Handel—Processional
Karg-Elert—All Depends on God's Blessing
Lohengrin—Wedding March
Marcello—The Heavens Declare the Glory
Purcell—Trumpet Tune
Widor—Nuptial March
Tombelle—March Pontificale

HYMNS

Cruger—Now Thank We All Our God
Neander—Praise Ye the Lord the Almighty
Zundel—Love Divine

LISTING OF OTHER SPECIALISTS

Suggestions of a number of professional organists and of people specializing in wedding music follow:

PRELUDES

Bach—Air for G String
    Air from Orchestral Suite in D Major
    Arioso in A Major
    In Thee Is Gladness
    Jesus, Joy of Man's Desiring
    Little G Minor, Cathedral, etc.
    Lord Jesus Christ Be Present Now
    Loving Jesus, We Are Here
    Now Thank We All Our God
    Our Father Who Art in Heaven
    See What His Love Can Do
Beethoven—Adagio
    Andante Cantabile from Symphony V
    Moonlight Sonata
Bennett—God Is a Spirit
Brahms—A Lovely Rose Is Blooming
Couperin—Benedictus
Diggle—Salut D'Amour
Dubois—Wedding "Mass," 5 selections
Franck—Cantabile
    Choral in A Minor
    Choral in B Minor
    Choral in E Major
    Pastorale
    Piece Heroique
Handel—Fireworks Music
    Water Music

Hokanson—Crown with Thy Benediction, or In Heavenly
    Love Abiding
Karg-Elert—Benedictus
Mendelssohn—But the Lord Is Mindful of His Own
    Hear My Prayer
Reger—Benedictus
Rheinberger—Cantilena
    Intermezzo from Sonata 17
    Vision
Smart—An Evening Prayer
Vierne—24 Pieces in Free Style
Widor—Slow Movements from Symphonies V and VI
Williams—Three Preludes on Welsh Tunes
Weaver—Bell Benedictus (Harp and Chimes)

WEDDING HYMNS

Jesus, Thou Joy of Loving Hearts (Quebec)
Now Thank We All Our God (Nun Danket)
Father, Loving Father (Livermore)
O God, Whose Love Is Over All (Denver)
May The Grace Of Christ Our Saviour (Stockwell)
Praise to the Lord, the Almighty (Lobe Den Herren)
In Heavenly Love Abiding (Seasons)
Praise, My Soul, the King of Heaven (Dulce Carmen)
Love Is Kind And Suffers Long (Capetown)
Love Divine, All Loves Excelling (Beecher)

VOCAL MUSIC

Bach—Jesus, Joy of Man's Desiring
    God, My Shepherd
    God, My Shepherd, Walks Beside Me
    My Heart Ever Faithful
Bach-Bunjes—Jesus, Shepherd, Be Thou Near Me
    O Love That Casts Out Fear
Bach-Diak—Trust in the Lord
Bitgood—The Greatest of These Is Love
Black—The Pledge
Brahms—Lord, Lead Us Still

Though I Speak with Tongues
Burleigh—O Perfect Love
Buxtehude—Lord, Who at Cana's Wedding Feast
    O Father, All Creating
Clokey—Set Me as a Seal
Davies—The Lord's My Shepherd
Dvorak—God Is My Shepherd
    I Will Sing New Songs of Gladness
Franck—O Lord Most Holy
Galbraith—Holy Spirit, Breath of Love
Gounod—Entreat Me Not to Leave Thee
Grieg—Ich Liebe Dich (I Love Thee)
Handel—Largo (Wedding Lyrics)
    Thanks Be to Thee
    Where Ere You Walk
Helder-Bunjes—The Lord My Shepherd Is
Hildack—Where'er Thou Goest
Kiecker-Wick—Bless Our Vows
Kittel—O Father, Son and Holy Ghost
LaForge—Father, Guide and Defend Us
Lippe—How Do I Love Thee
Lloyd—O Christ Who Once Hast Deigned
Lovelace—We Lift Our Hearts to Thee
Mendelssohn—The Voice That Breathed O'er Eden
Mozart—Alleluja
Polack—The Lord Be with You
Root—Love Never Faileth
Rowley—A Wedding Prayer
Trew—Brother James' Air
Thiman—Thou Wilt Keep Him in Perfect Peace
Vaughan Williams—The Call
Willan—Eternal Love
Wood—God Made Thee Mine
(by any of the following: Burleigh, Clokey, Clough-
    Leighter, Pedrette, Fox, Willan, Sowerby, Overby,
    or Barnby)—
    O Perfect Love

PROCESSIONALS

Bach—Adagio in A Minor
    Adagio (Toccata, Adagio and Fugue in C)
    Air (Orchestral Suite in D Major)
    Allebreve in D
    Arioso in A
    Sheep May Safely Graze
    Sinfonia (Wedding Cantata 196)
Biggs—Bell Symphony
Bloch—Four Wedding Marches
Clarke—Processional March
Clokey—Processional (A Wedding Suite)
    Recessional (A Wedding Suite)
Costa—Triumphal March
Dubois—Psalm XVIII
Grieg—March Triumphant
Handel—A Trumpet Voluntary
    Processional in G Minor
    Solemn Processional
Kreckel—Nuptial Procession
Mendelssohn—Allegro Mestoso (Sonata 4)
    Wedding March (Midsummer Night's Dream)
Purcell—Trumpet Tune
    Trumpet Tune in D Major
    Trumpet Voluntary in D
Purvis—Jubilate Deo
Stanley—Processional in G Major
    Trumpet Tune
Vierne—Carillon (24 Pieces in Free Style)
    Finale (Symphonie 1)
Wagner—Traditional Processional (Lohengrin)
Wesley—Choral Song
Widor—Toccata (Fifth Symphony)

RECESSIONALS

Dubois—Grand Choeur
Widor—Selected Movements Symphonies V & VI

IV. Premarital Counseling

The minister must conceive of his duty as more than merely conducting a wedding service. He is more than a "marrying Sam" or the church's "justice of the peace," who performs in a cold, uninterested manner, with his primary concern the size of the fee.

The minister's interest stretches far beyond the ceremony, to the couple's years of home and family life. Hence, his responsibility is to counsel the couple regarding all the factors involving happy marriage, so that a strong bond is cemented.

THE REASONS FOR PREMARITAL COUNSELING

"An ounce of prevention is worth a pound of cure" underscores the necessity for premarital counseling. A few interviews before the wedding, conferring frankly and confidentially with the prospective bride and groom, may well prevent numerous difficulties and heartaches. One counselor stated: "I'd rather have thirty minutes with a couple before marriage than ten hours after the die is cast. It's more effective."

Dr. Roy A. Burkhart, pastor of the First Community Church, Columbus, Ohio, said: "It is my practice not to marry a couple without going through a process of study with them. The number of premarital interviews with a couple will depend largely on the degree of insight they show, their questions, and their interest. I ordinarily have three one-hour interviews with a couple before marriage and one subsequent to marriage. The first three are in my study. The fourth is in the couple's home after their marriage." He has found the results to be so fruitful that he

43

proposed: "A program of guidance . . . should be provided by every church, not only to meet its fullest ministry but also its choicest opportunity. . . ."

Premarital counseling provides the opportunity for establishing good relationships in a prospective marriage. Questions frequently focus on personality adjustments, personality differences, wedding plans, the honeymoon, physical adjustments, housing plans, religious differences, money and its management, emancipation from family, adjustments to new friendships, and in-laws.

Premarital counseling gives counselees the opportunity to ventilate fears, doubts, and wishes regarding marriage and each other, so that they recognize the importance of inner feelings in a marital relationship.

Premarital counseling assists the couple to build and strengthen a realistic, positive philosophy toward marriage. By encouraging the couple to discuss their basic values, the minister aids them to realize that no marriage is perfect, and that all marriages require effort, compromise, unselfishness, and adjustment.

Premarital counseling should help determine the physical, intellectual, psychological, social, and spiritual compatibility of the couple and the potentials for happiness. If the situation indicates unusual or abnormal conditions, the minister may make referral to other specialists or agencies for assistance, or at least acquaint the couple with the professional resources available. He may discourage the couple from proceeding with marriage plans, and thus eliminate the possible later tragedy of divorce.

PREMARITAL COUNSELING PROGRAM

There can never be a stereotyped program of premarital counseling for all ministers. Perhaps no two ministers use the same methods in detail. One minister may feel quite unprepared to undertake any extended program, and will do little more than attempt a short talk with the couple. Another may offer a full course of guidance, including numerous hours of counseling and batteries of tests. Some ministers refuse to marry couples who are not willing to complete the procedure they outline; the average minister, however, is not so exacting in his demands.

Scheduling two or three sessions with the couple is the most common practice. There are exceptions, where persons come to the minister wishing to be married at once. Unless the minister refuses to perform the ceremony, he can do little more than talk with them a few minutes, offering helpful advice, giving them booklets for further reading, and creating a climate of friendliness that will open the door for subsequent counseling. If a minister refuses to marry such people, in all probability they will seek out a justice of the peace, the minister thereby forfeiting the church's chance to counsel and guide them during their married life.

A variety of premarital counseling methods and devices may be used by the minister, including: interviews, written materials, psychological tests, films, group counseling, and referrals.

Interviews

The interview, the main method used by the marriage counselor, is a process by which the minister helps the couple talk about, feel about, and work through various areas of consideration, until they can objectively make their own decisions and plans.

Various schools of thought exist regarding the best method of interviewing. The "client-centered" (nondirective) and "counselor-centered" (directive) approaches are two that are common. In the *directive* method it is assumed that the couple confers with an expert, who listens to questions and answers them, or who listens to problems, interprets, and then offers possible solutions, making definite recommendations.

The *nondirective* approach is based on the philosophy that the counselees do the work, and solve their own problems. The couple is asked questions, which they discuss in the presence of a sympathetic listener, the counselor. The purpose is to make them better understand themselves and their feelings, and more clearly chart their course.

Most ministers probably use the *eclectic* approach, a combination of the directive and nondirective approaches in interviewing. Most ministers feel that the personalities and demeanor of the counselees should determine the approach, and that versatility is desirable.

The minister's role should be that of an experienced friend who is vitally interested in the welfare and happiness of the counselees. He seeks to enter into their thoughts, feelings, and plans. He does not assume a lecturing role, giving good advice; rather, he seeks to stimulate them to express themselves and ask questions.

The marriage-counseling kit is a card-sorting device that serves as an icebreaker for couples who are being counseled, and determine their opinions regarding marriage.

Written Materials

One of the most common tools of counseling used by the minister is written material. A young couple, with the wedding date set, may be concerned about the physical side of marriage. The minister may talk with them about their questions and concerns, and then suggest two or three books that will give appropriate information.

Certain values are compromised and also there are inherent hazards involved in the use of written materials in counseling. The counselor should be well acquainted with the literature he recommends so that he knows it is worthwhile and so that he is prepared for subsequent discussions that may arise from the reading. The books recommended should be individualized, taking into consideration the intellectual capacity, emotional stability, and readiness of the persons involved. People often take home printed literature, but fail to read it, or ignore the unpleasant parts or that which is contrary to their beliefs. It is highly desirable for interviews to parallel the reading, so that the counselees have the opportunity to clarify their thinking and feelings regarding what is read.

A bibliography of appropriate literature is provided (p. 157) in the hope that it will be helpful in premarital counseling.

Psychological Tests

There are differences of opinion regarding the use of psychometric testing devices in marriage counseling. Although they have many limitations, they can be used to advantage. There is an educational effect on the couple, realized from their considering many significant factors relating to their personalities and marriage. Problems may be located which might otherwise be overlooked. An over-all view of marital potentials and needed adjustments are made more apparent. Among the tests recommended are: "Marriage Prediction Tests," by Burgess, Cottrell, and Terman; "Mate Selection Test," by Gilbert Appelhof; "Johnson Temperament Analysis"; "Bernreuter Test"; "Minnesota Multiphasic Test"; "California Personality Test"; "Guilford-Zinn Temperament Survey"; and "Augustana Premarital Scoring Device." One of the most complete and most satisfactory testing instruments for personality inventory and marriage-happiness prediction is James R. Hine's manual, *Grounds for Marriage*. It is in easily usable form, and is highly recommended for the minister's use. Although the statistical findings do not always apply to every individual case, yet, as the counselor interprets and discusses the various responses to the tests, they take on added meaning when impending marriage is considered. The minister must exercise caution, lest the tests lead to advice-giving.

Films

Several new audio-visuals, carefully designed by experts in the marriage-counseling field, are helping ministers in their counseling sessions. Two new 16-mm. color films have been released by the Broadcasting and Film Commission of the National Council of Churches. *Before They Say I Do* is a film for ministers about premarital counseling that should not be used with the counselees; it demonstrates the necessary skills for the minister and the pitfalls to be avoided. Its subject matter is primarily sex, attitudes toward sex, family planning, and methods of birth control. *I Do* is the other film, planned specifically for couples about to be married and for gatherings of young people of senior-high or college age. It is suitable for situations where the subject of marriage is to be discussed. *I Do* also centers on the sexual side of marriage. While it does not detail birth-control methods and the like, it pictures couples almost ready for marriage and presents with frankness their concerns about the marriage relationship. It pictures a clergyman counseling a girl of twenty who needs guidance and help. Each of these films has a running time of 28 minutes, and can be secured on a rental basis or purchased for $175.

Broader in scope is an excellent "Marriage Counseling Kit" of four color-soundstrips released by Family Films of Hollywood, prepared by Dr. Wayne E. Oates and Dr. Samuel Southard, selling for $25.50. Each filmstrip requires about 12 minutes for showing, one for each of four different counseling sessions. *Marriage Makes a Difference* highlights the difference between courtship and marriage. Its purpose is to help couples considering marriage to understand the new roles and responsibiilties they will be expected to assume. It includes matters to be considered by a couple during engagement, ways the church can help newlyweds, and suggestions for keeping romance alive. *Marriage Requires Adjustment* outlines some of the compromises and adjustments required by marriage: relationships to parents, where to live, whether the wife should continue to work, religious differences, money matters, finding oneness in marriage, and the part religion plays in making such adjustments. *The Intimacies of Marriage* deals forthrightly with sex in marriage and the importance of physical harmony. It pictures possible obstacles to sexual happiness in marriage, presents practical Christian ways to handle such obstacles, and indicates the contributions effective sex life can give to Christian marriage. *Making Marriage Last* is the concluding strip in the set. It deals with the "happily ever after" part practically and helpfully, how to grow in devotion to each other, making new friends in a new community, sharing family decisions, and developing religious faith as a couple.

Group Counseling

Organizing small groups or classes under skilled leadership has proved to be an effective way of helping prospective husbands and wives prepare for marriage. Group counseling provides an opportunity to work through fears and hostilities, releasing any conflicts in feelings. Release is accomplished through discussion, ventilation of feelings, as well as through "passive" participation (feeling deeply as the conflicts of others are heard). The necessary insight and support to reshape attitudes, modify behavior, deal with problems in new ways, and accomplish the necessary personality growth for more satisfactory marriage adjustment may result from this process.

The minister may be able, also, in his Sunday sermons to help persons preparing for marriage.

Referrals

One effective function of the minister-counselor is giving a referral to another qualified person and helping the counselee understand and accept the referral.

Among those to whom referrals may be made are: physician, lawyer, professional marriage counselor, and psychiatrist or marriage-counseling center.

During the initial interview the minister should suggest that the persons planning marriage have an interview with a *physician*. The minister can make the couple aware of the possible benefits of the physician's interview and delineate the areas about which they should inquire, such as: complete medical examination of both partners, including gynecological and urological, and a careful, non-traumatizing pelvic examination of the girl; blood analyses, including blood count, RH typing, and blood serology; discussion of factors contributing to adequate and satisfactory sexual adjustment; planned-parenthood information, if desired; discussion of hereditary concerns; discussion of anatomy and physiology of the reproductive system; sound information to dispel distorted ideas and reduce fears regarding childbirth; and proper referral if special attention is needed by a gynecologist, urologist or neurologist.

Usually, young couples marrying for the first time have no reason to seek *legal counsel*. However, there are cases of handling private income, legacies, wills, and property which might require legal assistance. In the event of unusual circumstances regarding the legality of a marriage due to foreign citizenship, race, or relationship, the minister would be wise to make a referral to a lawyer.

In cases of remarriage, there may be legal problems concerning the previous marriage, spouse, or children. Older persons remarrying, or even marrying for the first time, frequently have property, possessions, businesses, or other assets which they want to transfer, divide, or will in a specific manner. The lawyer is in a position to assist in premarital counseling, and thus prevent unhappiness and serious family complications in years ahead.

Many cities of America are blessed with *marriage-counseling centers*. Although their main function is to assist couples who are already married and have marital difficulties, they also provide premarital assistance. Usually there are several persons who represent different special services who are available for counsel.

If the minister recognizes abnormal emotional problems related to courtship and marriage, personality conflicts, or symptoms of neurosis or psychosis, a direct referral to a psychiatrist for evaluation or consultation is expedient. In some cases, the psychiatrist and minister may collaborate, with joint interviews and consultation, for the reorganization of the inner lives of the prospective mates.

AREAS TO BE COVERED

There are many areas of information that need to be covered for a successful premarital-counseling program. No fixed outline can be predetermined for every couple, however, for the minister's degree of knowledge of each will vary, plus the fact that the needs of each person will vary. It is not possible for the pastor to plan exactly what will be said in the counseling session; he must be ready for anything. Nevertheless, by proper lead-questions, the minister can direct conversations to the basic issues which most couples should confront before marriage. Among the areas that should be discussed are: degree of compatibility; the maturity of love; religious backgrounds; sex adjustment and birth-control information; finances.

Degree of Acquaintance and Compatibility

Research studies have shown that marriages preceded by long acquaintance have a much better chance of success than those of persons who marry hastily. Without thorough acquaintance, it can be little more than a guess whether there is a reasonable assurance of compatibility of temperament and personality. Persons who have known each other for a long time have probably already made many of the major adjustments of personality necessary.

Premarital counseling should determine whether the prospective partners have the similar tastes, wishes, habits, and ideals sufficient to provide a broad basis of understanding and enduring companionship; whether they enjoy the same pursuits, have the same interests, and are able to appreciate the same friends; whether they know how to disagree without unkindness, control their anger, and find

true harmony of spirit and respect in spite of differences.
A broad base of mutuality can be developed, providing the
two people want the same things from life and are willing
to go in the same direction. The main problems of adjustment should become apparent in the counseling process.

The Maturity of Love

While love is the greatest thing in marriage, it is far
deeper and more inclusive than many seeking marriage
realize. If love is interpreted only as a sentimental feeling,
then it will die when the romantic glamor fades. If it is
only physical attraction, then it will fade when the body
loses its beauty.

What does love involve for each marriage partner? What
is the concept of love? Have the persons gone beyond
mere infatuation? Have they achieved a creative partner-
ship?

Answers to these questions the minister should seek to
have expressed; he should emphasize that marriage is a
process of growth together, and that love grows deeper
and more profound as the years pass. In mature love, one
has the habit of thinking of the other more than of "self."

Religious Backgrounds

Among the most important explorations in premarital
interviewing are the religious backgrounds and intentions
of the two persons. Couples that are bound together in
God and in common religious experiences have a stability
that is not known to those whose marriages are based
merely on secular attitudes. The prospect for a happy and
enduring marriage is three times greater when both persons
are actively associated with the church. The emotions that
urge people into marriage are in danger of withering unless
they have strong roots in the entire nature of the individual—physical, mental, and spiritual.

The minister should make sure that persons from diverse
religious backgrounds understand the differences involved

and the potential difficulties that may arise; this is especially true when the persons involved are of Roman Catholic and Protestant, Christian and Jewish, and Christian and secular backgrounds. He should lead them to see how religion will bless and help their marriage, as well as how their home can be a cell in God's Kingdom on earth. The minister should help the couple work toward a common church affiliation before marriage, if at all possible. They may wish to attend the church of the person who is most active, or they may find it difficult to decide between churches since both are equally committed. Theirs will be a new family, distinct and unique. The agreement on church affiliation needs to be made, based not only on the religious patterns of the homes from which they have come, but also on consideration of the welfare of the new home. It should be a mutually agreeable solution, which may require a spirit of "compromise" by both persons in order to find a mutually acceptable church. The important factor is that they recognize in religious faith and practice a means of deeper communion with each other.

The minister should help them to recognize that God is the author and sustainer of the love which binds man and wife together.

Sex Adjustment

Some ministers believe that the subject of sex should receive the major attention in premarital counseling. It is true that sex is a basic and important element in marriage. Satisfactory physical adjustments and wholesome attitudes toward sex are essential for mental, social, and spiritual adjustments. Some attention does need to be given this subject in counseling in order that fears may be allayed or correct and proper information given. The sex relationship in Christian marriage is not the mere expression of physical passion and biological necessity. It is the symbol of the complete dedication of a man and woman to each other. It is an expression of self-giving and trust. It is the part of one's value system which demonstrates the inner essence of marriage. It is appropriate for the minister to deal with the sex relationship as part of spiritual unity and self-giving in marriage. There is much ignorance, erroneous information, prudishness, and gratification-seeking that contribute to maladjustment. Although this subject need not be the main, or only, subject of premarital counseling, it must not be treated artifically or neglected, with the assumption that any adjustment will be made automatically.

Some ministers feel that the treatment of this question can be done best through printed material, carefully chosen and perhaps given by the minister, with a brief explanation.

Still other ministers feel that the sexual aspect of marriage can be better and more normally handled by a well-chosen physician, who can determine the physical elements of fitness and can assist in giving birth-control advice.

Finances

One of the most difficult adjustments for the newly married may be financial. A large number of marital problems (that confront the author, at least) have some relationship to money. Usually, each unmarried person has the habit of making his or her own decisions regarding the spending of money, perhaps with no conscious budget limitations. In marriage, however, there must be teamwork, and an unselfish consideration of each other. The financial problem is not always that there is an insufficient amount of money to spend; it is more often a question of common purpose, of wise spending, of curbing selfishness, and of using money in such a way that each will feel that the other is considerate.

The minister can encourage a plan for setting up a budget in order to avoid financial misunderstandings and difficulties. The couple has to achieve agreement about what they want, how to plan for it, and how to spend.

Decisions should be made regarding whether the wife should work, what sort of insurance program they should start, whether they should purchase on credit, whether there is sufficient income to get started, who should pay the bills, and what kind of bank account to open.

I counsel husbands and wives to have separate, individual bank accounts. To provide access to each other's accounts in case of emergency, each can give the other either a limited or a full power of attorney. Some persons say: "My wife and I trust each other, so we have a joint bank account. It is a symbol of our unity." Fine. However, the joint account, technically, has inherent difficulties that may not be recognized. In the case of the death of one party to the account, the other party may be barred from any access to it until it has been released by the state in which the bank is located. The state's tax agents want to make sure they collect full inheritance taxes on such accounts, and, far from assuming that the account belongs to the survivor, they are likely to take the position that it belonged entirely to the decedent and is therefore fully subject to tax. Not all the defects of a joint account are postmortem. Each party to the account must keep the other aware of all deposits and all checks drawn, or it is not possible to keep track of the balance on hand.

EXAMPLES OF PREMARITAL COUNSELING PROCEDURES

Procedures for premarital counseling are as varied as the number of ministers. Each has a different manner, and usually develops his own techniques, adapting them to the needs of the particular couple he is interviewing. It is desirable to have several unhurried periods to evaluate a particular method, and to know the procedures of other ministers who excel in this area.

George C. Desmond

George C. Desmond,[1] minister of the Methodist Church, uses four sessions. At the first session, the couple meets with him to arrange a date and schedule for the ceremony and rehearsal, and to receive information concerning the necessary preparations. During this session, the minister presents a booklet, *Wedding Etiquette,* by Jabez Taylor. He reads the wedding ceremony with the couple, and discusses its meaning, phrase by phrase. Then he talks about the deeper, spiritual meanings of married life; the need for understanding the sexual relationship; the need for agreeing on finances; and various other problems and areas of tension that should be recognized. He loans or gives the couple two books, to be read before the next session: *Harmony in Marriage,* by Wood and Dickinson, and *Sexual Harmony in Marriage,* by Butterfield. The second and third sessions are with the prospective bride and groom, respectively. During these sessions, the minister establishes a deep, personal rapport. He follows up the reading assignments in the books loaned, and discusses any subject which may be raised. The final session is held with both together. Its purpose is for the discussion of any questions about which the couple needs more information. The pastor gives brief, meaningful advice, and talks seriously about the sacredness of married life. A prayer concludes the session.

Oliver M. Butterfield

Dr. Oliver M. Butterfield[2] gives a list of questions to the persons to be married. From this, he asks them to select those which they would like to talk about. His list is as follows:

1. How long acquainted? Where did you meet? How well acquainted?
2. How do your families feel about the match?
3. Where do you expect to live after marriage?
4. What are your business connections? Ambitions? Permanence? Will the wife work after marriage? How long?
5. Have you agreed on a practical budget? Who will keep the books?

6. Does either of you carry life insurance?
7. Has either of you health problems to face? How long since you had physical examinations? Do you plan to have examinations before marriage?
8. Social life and recreation—Do you have the same set of friends in general? Does either of you dislike some of the other's friends? What amusements or hobbies do you have in common? Separately? How do you get on with each other's relatives?
9. Home life and plans—How do you agree on likes and dislikes in food? Music? Clothes (color schemes, etc.)? Have you ambitions to own your own home?
10. Sex information and reading—What have you read on the sexual aspects of marriage? Would you like the name of a reliable physician whom you could consult if you wished to do so? Are you agreed about children? Do you have reliable information on birth control?
11. Miscellaneous inquiries—Anxieties about problems of differences in temperament, heredity, age, education, religion, family dominance, travel.
12. Religious life and attitudes—What were the religious habits and attitudes of your parents? Do you personally differ from your parents in such matters? What are your plans for religious life after marriage?
13. Dismissal, with some plan for subsequent contacts.

James R. Hine

Dr. James R. Hine,[3] who recently developed, at the McKinley Foundation, Danville, Illinois, new help for couples preparing for marriage, suggests in his excellent book, *Grounds for Marriage,* having seven interviews as follows:

1. The first period is consumed in filling out the "Details of Wedding Form" and the "Marriage Information Record" (see pp. 31 and 61, respectively); surveying the planning book *Your Wedding Workbook,* by Belting and Hine, assigning reading in *Harmony in Marriage,* by Wood and Dickinson, and the "What You Bring to Marriage"

chapter of *Grounds for Marriage*, by Hine. Also, the *Marriage Counseling Kit* cards can be used effectively (see Bibliography).

2. During the second period, the couple receives and discusses the contents of the previous assignments. Then work is begun on other sections of *Grounds for Marriage:* "Adventure Into Mutuality," and "Exploring Habits, Interests, and Ideas."

3. In session three, the materials assigned in the second session are discussed, plus the remainder of *Harmony in Marriage*. The couple is assigned to read the section in *Grounds for Marriage* on "Personality Traits Composed" and the "Inventory Charts," to work on "Facing the Home and the Future," and to read *Handbook for Husbands and Wives*, by Arden, or *Sexual Harmony in Marriage*, by Butterfield.

4. Period four is spent reviewing and discussing the completed assignments from session three. This is a good time for the couple to take the "Sex Knowledge Inventory Test" in *Grounds for Marriage*. Also, a check of the progress in *Your Wedding Workbook* is made.

5. In session five, the couple faces the important decision of religion in marriage. The chapter "Religious Homes Are Happy Homes" in *Grounds for Marriage* is discussed. The wedding ceremony is read, pausing for interpretation and discussion of meaning. All the details of *Your Wedding Workbook* are checked.

6. The wedding practice and the final pre-wedding interview comprise the sixth session. The couple is asked to bring the *Wedding Workbook*.

7. Seven weeks after the wedding, the clergyman makes a friendly visit to the couple's home, discussing their marriage in the light of the interviewing time.

DISSUADING MARRIAGE

In some cases, the minister will feel it necessary to dissuade people from marrying. Especially is this true when: the couple is very young; the plan to marry seems hasty and ill-considered; the persons are openly profane or drunk; there is serious emotional instability, or a high incidence of mental disease in the families, or active tuberculosis or venereal disease; medical examinations reveal that for some reason normal sex relations will not be possible. The minister cannot sidestep these factors, or just hope that no difficulties will arise. He has a responsibility to the persons themselves, to society, and to his own conscience.

Dissuading marriage is a difficult matter. It is doubtful that the minister ought to conclude dogmatically and arbitrarily that the marriage cannot succeed (the couple might prove him wrong); however, he can express his concerns, and urge that they delay plans for marriage for further counsel and research, which might bring them to the conclusion that the union would be unwise. The minister might say: "In view of this unsolved problem, do you not think it would be better for all concerned to delay your marriage until you have been able to think these matters through?" The minister does a tragic disservice by marrying the obviously mismated, and he does any couple a service by getting them to postpone an ill-considered step.

THE DIVORCEE SEEKING REMARRIAGE

Should a minister conduct the ceremony for a divorcee? This is becoming an increasingly prevalent problem because of the great number of divorcees, young and old.

In some denominations, the minister is refrained explicitly from remarrying divorcees by a specific law in his church. Some pastors have the personal policy of refusing to marry all divorced persons, it being a matter of conscience—to marry divorcees, they feel, would make them a party to violation of New Testament teaching.

However, others feel that this simple solution may involve a cruel injustice and is too arbitrary. It would seem to some that each case should be considered on its merits.

Admittedly, the Christian ideal is marriage for life; yet we live in an unideal world. Many mistakes and immature marriage decisions are made. Divorce, though sinful, is often the lesser of two evils. It is sinful, yet not unpardonable, wherein there is a humble, contrite spirit of remorse, and a genuine repentance.

The minister is concerned both to help the persons who come to him, and to maintain Christian standards. Where there has been a first failure, the minister should certainly not pass over the matter with the mere hope that the new venture will be more successful. Rather, by counseling, he should help the person who has made one domestic failure to understand the destructive factors which wrecked the first marriage, and to avoid such in the second. A divorced person should develop insight into the causes of the first failure, and determine to avoid such mistakes in the future, before even considering remarriage. When such a spirit is manifested by one seeking remarriage, and if sufficient time has elapsed for maturing and emotional freedom to develop, it might be very unwise for the church to close the door for a remarriage. It might be most spiritually damaging to one seeking recovery and an honorable life. Some ministers, therefore, without condoning divorce or considering it lightly, attempt to determine the factors which caused the divorce and whether the attitudes and habits which contributed to the first breakdown have been overcome, so as not to undo a second marriage. The minister should try to determine the sincerity, the maturity, and the depth of repentance of the party seeking remarriage before turning him or her away. In the spirit of prayer for God's guidance and His forgiveness, the decision can be made.

CLERGYMAN'S MARRIAGE INFORMATION AND PERMANENT RECORD[3]

Wedding of: Date of Application_____
_____ Time of Wedding_____
_____ Church or Chapel_____
File No._____   Officiating Clergyman_____

Preliminary question: "Has either of you been married before?"_____ (Note: In case of applicant's previous marriage, special arrangements must be made, due to Church laws.) (See p. 000 for further discussion.)

QUESTIONS TO ASK THE BRIDE

1. Full name of bride_____
2. Present address_____ Phone no._____
3. Residence after marriage_____
4. At what permanent address may you always be reached?_____
5. Occupation_____ Age_____
6. Place of birth_____
7. Father's name_____ Mother's maiden name_____
8. How would you classify the married life of your parents?
   Extremely happy_____ Moderately happy_____
   Satisfactory_____ Unsatisfactory_____
   Divorced_____
9. Church membership_____ Attend where?_____
   Active?_____
10. How long have you known the person you intend to marry?_____

11. How would you classify your parents' attitude toward your coming marriage?

Enthusiastic: Father_____ Mother_____

Favorable: Father_____ Mother_____

Mild approval: Father_____ Mother_____

Consent with reservations: Father_____ Mother_____

Object to marriage: Father_____ Mother_____

12. If there is an objection to the marriage, what are the grounds?_____

13. What factors lead you to believe you will have a happy married life together?_____

14. What preparation have you made for marriage by way of study courses, reading, or consultations with doctor, minister, or other counselor?_____

_____

15. When you see your doctor, will you have a thorough physical examination in preparation for marriage? _____ A talk with him?_____

QUESTIONS TO ASK THE GROOM

1. Full name of groom_____

2. Present address_____ Phone no._____

3. At what permanent address may you always be reached?_____

_____

4. Occupation_____ Age_____

5. Place of birth_____

6. Father's name_____ Mother's maiden name_____

7. How would you classify the married life of your parents?

Extremely happy_____ Moderately happy_____

Satisfactory_____ Unsatisfactory_____

Divorced_____

8. Church membership_____ Attend where?_____
9. How would you classify your parents' attitude toward your marriage?
   Enthusiastic: Father_____ Mother_____
   Favorable: Father_____ Mother_____
   Mild approval: Father_____ Mother_____
   Consent with reservations: Father_____ Mother_____
   Object to marriage: Father_____ Mother_____
10. If there is an objection to the marriage, what are the grounds?_____
    _____
11. What factors lead you to believe that you will have a happy married life together?_____
12. What preparation have you made for marriage by way of study courses, reading, or consultations with doctor, minister, or other counselor?_____
    _____
13. When you see a doctor, will you have a thorough physical examination in preparation for marriage? _____ A talk with him?_____

QUESTIONS TO ASK THE COUPLE
Are you willing to enter into a counseling program, which involves private study and at least two more interviews with the counselor?_____ Dates for further conferences_____

V. The Wedding Rehearsal

The best assurance of a beautiful and orderly wedding service is a thorough rehearsal.

It is generally necessary to have a rehearsal for every wedding that has a processional planned. The exception is the informal, "stand-up" wedding where no guests or only the immediate families are present. In the latter case, the minister usually can give brief instructions to the persons involved just prior to the wedding service.

TIME FOR REHEARSAL

The most common and effective time for the rehearsal usually is the night before the wedding. To have it prior to this time risks all the participants not being present, or those present forgetting some of the important details. To have the rehearshal on the day of the wedding is to overcrowd an already busy day for the bride and her party. When a wedding dinner is planned, it is most convenient to have the rehearsal prior to the dinner the night before the wedding; or the rehearsal may follow the dinner. One hour's time should be allowed for the rehearsal.

It is imperative that all participants be present and on time for the rehearsal, including the ushers, the parents of the bride and groom, and the musicians. It is the bride's responsibility to notify each person of the rehearsal time.

THE REHEARSAL DIRECTOR

The minister is in charge of the rehearsal instructions, unless a wedding counselor is hired. He should be the "take-charge" person, knowing the exact details, being discreet, decisive, and thorough. Occasionally, the bride may want a florist, a wedding specialist, or her mother to conduct the rehearsal. Generally, such practices are discouraged because they can lead to confusion, unless there is prior clearing of details with the minister. It is a much better practice for the processional details to be discussed with the minister and decisions made during one of the pre-wedding conferences, so that the minister can direct the rehearsal with decisiveness. If there are alternate ideas projected during the rehearsal, it can be confusing to the participants. The minister should give attention to every detail, taking nothing for granted, so that every person knows what is expected of him and when. In some of the large congregations, where the demands upon the minister's time are many, a wedding hostess may be assigned to direct rehearsals for him. She, of course, would be trained in the details and procedures used by the minister.

THE WEDDING-SERVICE PLAN

A list of participants should be prepared by the bride and handed to the minister prior to the rehearsal.

When the participants have arrived for the rehearsal, the minister should invite all to the front of the sanctuary, and ask that they be seated. He then introduces himself and the organist, greets the members of the wedding party, and announces the wedding procedure.

The minister should announce the wedding-service plan and time at the outset of the rehearsal.

A generally accepted procedure is: prelude music (to begin 15 minutes prior to announced time); seating of guests by ushers; candles lighted; groom's parents ushered to seats; bride's mother ushered to seat; aisle runner unrolled; vocal music; the wedding processional; the marriage ceremony; the wedding recessional; bride's parents ushered out; groom's parents ushered out; congregation dismissed.

Slight alterations can be made in this procedure in accord with local policy, practice, or desire.

The Ushering of Guests

Much of the smooth orderliness depends upon the usher's finesse and alertness. Therefore, the ushers should be given thorough instructions.

Ushers should arrive one hour in advance of the wedding time, to see that the proper lights are on, the doors are opened, the flowers are distributed, and early guests are seated. Each woman guest is extended the right arm by the usher and taken to a seat; husbands and children follow. Men who attend without women companions are led to seats. The first or second row of the two center sections is reserved for the mothers and fathers of the bride and groom. Other relatives are seated in the rows immediately in back of the parents—the bride's relatives on the left side and the groom's on the right, facing the chancel. The florist identifies the proper number of rows reserved by decorating with special ribbons. The ushers inquire of each guest: "Are you a relative of the bride or groom?" If an affirmative answer is given, he is seated in the proper reserved section; if not, the guest is seated in the sanctuary.

The grandparents usually are not seated until just before the mothers are, and immediately behind or beside the parents.

Lighting of the Candles

At the appropriate time, the candlelighters walk together from the rear of the sanctuary, carrying the lighters. In the event that one goes out, it can be lighted from the other. The candlelighters begin from the outside of the candelabra, lighting the candles one by one, in unison. When all are lighted, they meet at the center and extinguish the lighters. If they are ushers, they then proceed to the rear of the sanctuary; if not, they are seated in the front row, one to the far left and the other to the far right.

Seating the Mothers

Following the candle-lighting, the groom's mother, followed by the father, is ushered to the first or second row on the right side. The bride should select the ushers whom she wishes to escort the mothers. The bride's mother is then seated in the first or second row on the left side, facing the chancel. During the ceremony, the ushers stand at the rear of the sanctuary, unless they are involved as groomsmen as well.

SEATING CHARTS

Church With Center Aisle

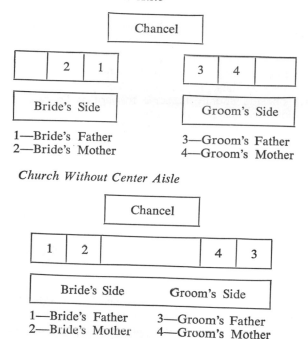

Church Without Center Aisle

The Aisle Cloth

In the more formal weddings, an aisle cloth is used for the processional party. If the sanctuary has several aisles, the center aisle is roped off until the processional, and the white aisle cloth is laid in advance. Guests are ushered down the side aisles.

When the processional aisle has to be used for guests, the aisle cloth is either rolled or folded at the foot of the chancel steps until the processional is to begin. Following the seating of the mothers, the cloth is laid. If it is on a roller, the usher who seats the bride's mother may unroll the aisle cloth as he returns to the rear of the sanctuary. If the cloth is folded, two ushers are needed, each taking a corner and unfolding it as they move to the back of the church.

Processional Instructions

It is usually best to begin the rehearsal by giving instructions to those in the procession. The minister asks each one individually to come forward as he calls their position, and places them where they will stand for the beginning of the ceremony. Care should be taken that the spacing is proper (see diagrams, pp. 70–1), and that each person makes a mental note of his position in relationship to the chancel steps and others in the party. While all are in their places, the minister explains about the door from where each will come, the spacing, the kind of walk, and how they will stand while the bride and her father process.

As a general rule, the groom, best man, and minister enter the sanctuary from a side front door, following the wedding-march call. They walk slowly, erectly, and approximately four feet apart. The groomsmen may come from this location as well; from the rear of the sanctuary, by twos; or each groomsman may escort a bridesmaid. The bride should make the choice of which way this should be done prior to the rehearsal, so that there is no question. When the men reach their positions at the chancel steps, they face toward the center aisle, with hands either at the sides or folded in front, with left over right (this should be consistent with all the male attendants). The men should have pleasant smiles as they watch the bridesmaids, maid of honor, and bride process to the altar.

The first bridesmaid enters the sanctuary from the rear of the church at the conclusion of the wedding-march call, followed by the other bridal attendants, who should be spaced approximately twelve to twenty feet apart. It is helpful to have a "starter," to space the girls properly— this may be the pastor's wife, the florist, or the church hostess. Each girl walks slowly, in time with the music.

The bride and her father hesitate at the head of the center aisle, so that her train may be straightened by the "starter," and the organist can time the beginning with a joyous crescendo. The bride and her father, who is on her left, begin with their left foot, and keep in step. The father must remember to keep to the side of the aisle so that the bride (usually wearing a bouffant gown) has ample room, and the father does not walk or trip on the dress.

As the bride arrives at the chancel, she should come to the center of the aisle and stop directly in front of the minister, about two steps away. The music promptly fades out.

After these instructions are given, the participants are sent to the rooms from which they will enter, the organist is given the signal, and a walk-through rehearsal of the processional is started. Special attention should be given the ring-bearer and the flower girl, if there be such. Young children can become frightened or can unconsciously distract from the sacredness of a wedding. Many humorous, yet unfortunate, happenings have been related regarding the actions and activities of children in wedding parties; hence, their participating can justifiably be discouraged. If they are a part of the party, it might be wise to have the best man responsible for the ring-bearer, and the maid of honor for the flower girl.

DIAGRAMS OF ARRANGEMENTS

Key to Diagrams —

A, altar or prie-dieu; M, minister; G, groom; BM, best man; U, ushers; BM, bridesmaids; MH, maid (or matron) of honor; FG, flower girl or pages; RB, ring-bearer; BF, bride's father; B, bride.

Possible Processional Arrangements

Plan 1

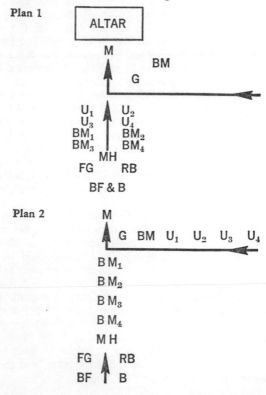

Plan 3

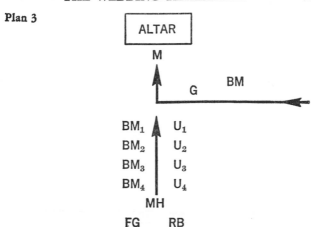

Possible Arrangements at the Chancel Steps

Plan 1

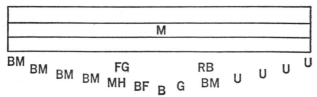

Plan 2

Plan 3

Possible Arrangements at Prie-Dieu

Plan 1

Plan 2

Plan 3

Possible Recessional Arrangements

Plan 1

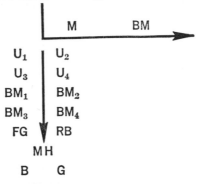

Plan 2

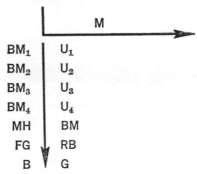

Escorting Mothers Out

Details of the Ceremony

In order for the service to proceed smoothly and to eliminate confusion, it is essential that all details be considered beforehand.

It is important to remind the participants that the wedding is a sacred worship service, to be conducted with dignity, reverence, and order. No one should chew gum. Attention should be focused upon the one officiating, with no wandering of eyes nor distracting movements. During prayers, members of the wedding party bow their heads.

At the proper time, the minister asks in similar words: "Who giveth this woman to be the bride of this man?" Whereupon the bride's father, with his left hand, may take her right hand, approach the minister one step, place her hand in the minister's, and say, "Her mother and I do," or "I do." For the bride's right hand to be free for this necessitates her dropping her father's arm immediately upon arrival at the chancel, and transferring her bouquet from the right to the left hand. After this he is seated by the bride's mother and next to the aisle. (The details here may vary according to the minister's wishes.) When the bride approaches the minister, she moves slightly to her left, so that as she and the groom are asked to join right hands, he steps forward to her side and stretches forth his right hand, and the minister can gently place the bride's hand on his.

It is helpful for the groom and bride to know that the wedding pledge is composed of a series of questions, so that when it is directed to each personally, they will not respond until the end. The minister should assure them that he will have an inflection in his voice. At the rehearsal it is helpful for the closing phrase to be recited, so that each will know his and her cue to answer "I will." In some ceremonies the correct response is "I do"; however, "I will" is perferred by most denominations because it carries the connotation of permanency. The answer should be given clearly.

For the ring exchange and vows, the bride and groom, maid of honor, and best man move from the chancel steps to the prie-dieu (or altar). The minister turns and takes his place behind the prie-dieu, which is the signal for the four to move forward. The groom assists the bride up the steps. They drop hands, however, upon reaching their stations, about two feet in front of the prie-dieu, so that the bride may transfer her flowers to the maid of honor at the appropriate time.

The best man has, or gets from the ring-bearer, the bride's ring, and gives it to the minister when requested. The maid of honor does likewise with the groom's ring. When the rings are placed, care must be taken to put them on the proper finger of the left hand. If the bride wears gloves, the left-hand, third finger of the glove should be cut or the glove removed for the ring exchange. The bride removes her engagement ring prior to the service and wears it on her right hand. If the ring does not slip easily over the knuckle, it should be left at the knuckle for the time being, rather than struggle with it; later, it can be forced on. The bride and groom should say their vows to one another. In some ceremonies, the vows are memorized; in others, each repeats after the minister the phrases of the wedding vows. If the ring is dropped accidentally, a spare should be ready, or the best man should be alerted to retrieve it, while all retain composure.

Most formal wedding ceremonies conclude with kneeling at the prie-dieu, during which time the benediction blessing is spoken or sung. The bride kneels first, with the assistance of the groom; after she is situated, he kneels. While kneeling, the back should be erect. The groom places his left hand over the bride's right hand on the upright of the prie-dieu; they support themselves with their outside hands.

Upon the conclusion of the benediction, after the "Amen" is said, the couple rises, and they face one another and prepare to kiss. The bride's veil is lifted to the top of her head either by the maid of honor or by the groom.

Discretion, brevity, and good judgment should be used in the kiss, which is a public seal of the covenant, and not a prolonged embrace of passion. A tender, brief kiss of affection is most appropriate.

As the couple turn to leave, following the kiss, the minister may, if he desires, say to the congregation: "I now present to you Mr. and Mrs. ———."

The Recessional

Following the wedding kiss, the organist begins the recessional music. The bride takes her husband's right arm, and they recess out the center aisle.

According to strictest etiquette, the maid of honor leaves alone, followed by the bridesmaids, by twos, and the groomsmen, by twos. The best man and minister then leave by the side door. The reason for this recessional order is that only the bride and groom are to be paired into a couple, and the others in the party have nothing particularly in common, and may even be complete strangers. However, the general custom is for the party to leave by pairing off—the maid of honor and best man, and each bridesmaid with a groomsman.

Dismissing the Congregation

Immediately following the recessional of the wedding party, the bride's mother is ushered out. Since the father is seated next to the aisle, the usher hesitates when approaching him, so that the bride's father can get out and take one step toward the chancel while the mother steps out and takes the usher's arm. If the bride's grandmother is present, the bride's father may usher her out as he leaves. The same procedure is followed in escorting the groom's mother.

If the attendance is large, the congregation should be ushered out two rows at a time. After ushering out the bride's and groom's mothers, the two ushers come to the front, and dismiss one row on each side simultaneously.

If the attendance is small, the minister remains at the prie-dieu until the parents are escorted out and then dismisses (with upraised hands) all of the congregation, or the head usher may come to the front of the center aisle and dismiss them with a similar gesture.

THE PHOTOGRAPHS

Picture taking during the wedding ceremony is discouraged or forbidden justifiably in most churches because it is a worship service, not a performance. Often, permission is given for one photograph at the rear of the sanctuary as the bride and father begin their procession, and one from the same location of the bride and groom, recessing. Posing for photographs may precede the reception if no more than fifteen minutes is absorbed; if a longer time than this is needed, the guests would become tired of waiting, and the photographs should follow the reception.

Good organization, cooperation, and speed must be exercised, to eliminate the prolonged standing of the guests who await the reception.

The usual pictures that are to be taken at this time are: total wedding party; bride, groom, maid of honor, and best man together; couple and minister; couple with both sets of parents; the couple; and the bride alone.

If the reception is in an adjacent room, two photographs should be taken of the cutting of the cake, and one of the bride serving the groom the first bite.

The bride should impress upon the photographer in advance the church's policy, the time limit, and the poses desired.

THE RECEPTION LINE

While the cake is being cut and the photographs are being taken, the reception line should be formed. Those composing the reception line usually are in the following order: bride's mother, groom's mother, bride's father, groom's father (fathers are optional), bride, groom, maid of honor, best man, bridesmaids, and groomsmen (optional).

VI.   Wedding Etiquette
the Minister Should Know

THE MINISTER'S WEDDING ATTIRE

Appropriate wedding dress for the minister varies with the church tradition, and possibly with the type and hour of wedding.

There is much to be said for wearing the robe vestment. Traditionally, it is distinctive for the clergy and sets him apart as the presiding person. It is tasteful and dignified, and lends reverence and sacredness to the occasion. The robe is appropriate for all wedding occasions, and relieves the clergyman from trying to match the attire of the male attendants. It covers the shirt, tie, and trousers, and hence is not distracting in any way.

For ministers who prefer not to wear a robe, or those whose tradition forbids such, the garb should be determined by the formality and time of the wedding. A formal wedding requires formal attire—this usually means a black tuxedo, with matching accessories of black shoes, socks, and bow tie; or, it may mean a white, single-breasted jacket with black tuxedo trousers. The minister should inquire at an early wedding conference what kind of garb, including the tie, is to be worn by the male attendants; then he plans to dress accordingly.

For an informal wedding in the morning or afternoon, or one held in the parish home, the minister may wear a dark business suit with conservative tie.

SECOND MARRIAGES

A second wedding for the bride usually should be more modest and less elaborate than the first. If it takes place after the death of the first mate or after a divorce is granted, the more quiet and informal the wedding the better. Usually it is discreet to invite only the close relatives and intimate friends.

The bride does not wear white nor a bridal veil on the occasion of a second marriage. She usually wears a street-length dress and hat.

Unless the family of her first husband deeply disapproves of her second mariage, a widow-bride sends them invitations to her second wedding. It is good taste for a widow to put away her first mate's engagement and wedding rings when she becomes engaged to marry for the second time.

If it is a second marriage for the groom, but the first for the bride, plans for a beautiful wedding should not be affected.

Young children of a first marriage, as a general rule, should not attend the second marriage of either parent, if there has been divorce. It is quite correct for children to attend if the parent is widowed. It is desirable for a parent wishing to remarry to seek his or her children's blessings and good wishes. Unless it is an obvious mismating, with ulterior motives, children should consent. If children of a previous mariage persistently resent the new marriage, it is desirable to forego a large wedding and to marry with only the necessary legal witnesses present.

When persons formerly divorced wish to be reunited to each other in marriage, no formal announcements should be sent out. However, friends are informed by letter or telephone. Often the children are involved.

WHEN PARENTS ARE DIVORCED

When a daughter lives with her mother, who is divorced from her father, the invitations are sent out in the mother's name. Her present husband's name may be included. Never do divorced parents send them out together. In such circumstances, it is better that the wedding be given by the mother; to do otherwise might imply that the mother had been unfit to have the custody of her daughter.

The bride's mother should be seated in the regular pew reserved for the bride's mother, with members of her family and her second husband, if she is remarried.

It is proper that the father walk up the aisle of the church with his daughter and give her away, even though the invitations are sent out by his former wife. He then takes his place in one of the pews further back on the bride's side. If remarried, he may be accompanied by his new wife. If relations are strained, some other male relative may give the bride away, or her mother might if her father is not to attend the wedding.

If the groom's parents are divorced, again, the mother and family should be given the regular pew on the groom's side of the church, and the father seated several rows behind on the same side.

Every effort should be made to make the meetings of the divorced parents friendly and not conspiciously tense. The bride or groom needs to feel that those who brought her or him into existence are on this day brought together peacefully because of their mutual concern for their offspring's happiness.

If the bride's remarried mother gives the reception, her husband acts as host, and the bride's father attends only as a guest. If the father gives the reception, and he has not remarried, he stands first in the line to receive guests. If he has remarried, his wife acts as hostess. If the bride's mother attends the reception under the latter circumstances, she is present as a guest, and should not stand at the side of her former husband nor share duties as hostess.

WHEN THE BRIDE'S MOTHER GIVES HER AWAY[1]

If the bride's father is dead, the bride's mother may give her away if a brother, an uncle, or some other male relative hasn't been selected for the honor. There are several ways this may be done—the bride's mother may walk down the aisle with her daughter, but not, of course, with the bride on her arm; the bride may walk in the processional with her brother or other male relative, her mother joining as she reaches the left front pew; sometimes the bride walks alone in the processional, and her mother joins her as she reaches her mother's pew; a male relative may escort the bride to the chancel steps, and, when the clergyman asks who is to give the bride away, the mother nods or stands to say "I do" from her traditional place or, just before the words are to be spoken, is escorted to the chancel by the best man, who steps down for the gesture. The latter is necessary only in those ceremonies (Episcopalian, for example) where the one who "gives the bride away" actually places her hand in the minister's.

POSTPONING A WEDDING, OR RECALLING INVITATIONS

When death occurs in the immediate family of the bride or groom, it is proper for the wedding to be postponed. If the death is of a very old person—a grandmother or grandfather—who has been ill, postponement is rarely called for. The action to be taken depends upon the feelings of the persons involved and the traveling distances required.

If the decision is made to postpone the wedding or to recall invitations for this or any other reason, the guests should be notified by telephone, wire, or, if time permits, by printed cards in the same style as the invitations.

THE DOUBLE WEDDING

Occasionally, sisters, cousins, or just close friends wish to marry at the same time in a double wedding. Such can be most meaningful, dramatic, and impressive. The double wedding need not be formal, nor with participants dressed alike.

In the double wedding, each bride and each groom usually have separate attendants, with the same number involved, and with harmonizing color schemes. Sometimes, sisters have the same attendants. The brides may act as maid and matron of honor for each other, and the grooms as best men for each other.

The ushers of both groups must be dressed identically, even when the bridesmaids' costumes differ for each bride. The only time that ushers may be dressed differently is when civilians and military men serve together. In a double wedding, all the ushers are paired according to height in the processional.

If the church has two interior aisles leading to the chancel, each bridal party may use a separate aisle, timing the entrance and exit together. The mothers of the brides and grooms are escorted up the respective aisles by ushers in the usual way just before the ceremony begins. The grooms' mothers are seated in the section to right of the aisles; the brides' mothers are seated in the section to the left of the aisles.

If the church has only a center aisle, with no other interior aisles, then the procession is up the center aisle. Both grooms' mothers are seated in the section to the right of the aisle, with the mother of the groom of the older bride using the front row, and the other groom's mother the next row. The brides' mothers are seated in the section to the left of the aisle, with the older bride's mother in the front row and the other mother in the second row. The party of the older bride processes first, followed by the party of the younger bride. If the girls are sisters, the father escorts the older girl, and a brother or other male relative escorts her sister. In the recessional, the elder bride, who has married first, leads down the chancel steps with her groom, and is followed by the younger bride with her groom. The attendants follow in the proper order, those of the first bride first, or paired with those of the second bride if an equal number makes it possible. Otherwise, they leave as they arrived.

THE HOME WEDDING

The home is a frequent setting for a wedding. If the wedding is large, the largest room is cleared, an altar is improvised at some focal point as far from the entrance as possible, and sections for the parents and relatives are roped off. When there is a staircase, the bride descends it when the wedding march is played. Otherwise, the bridal party congregates outside the entrance of the room before the music begins.

If the wedding is small, there may be no music at all, with participants dressed informally. The clergyman leads the wedding party to the place prepared for the ceremony.

A reception usually is given at a home wedding. It may be in the same room as that in which the wedding takes place, in the garden, or on a porch. A large table is usually moved against a wall, and set with the wedding cake as the central theme.

A wedding may take place out of doors if the climate is sufficiently dependable and if alternative arrangements have been made in case of inclement weather.

Receiving at a Home Wedding

At a home wedding, there is no recessional unless a formal receiving line is to form elsewhere in the house or in the garden. Where there are many guests and space is limited, the receiving line, if there is to be one, is best located in a small room such as a hall or dining room with both exit and entrance to facilitate the steady flow of traffic. Guests should be able to pass on into a larger area, where they may congregate and have refreshments. In simple home weddings, it is usual for the bride and groom merely to turn around at the altar after the benediction and kiss, to receive congratulations.

THE WEDDING IN A CLERGYMAN'S FAMILY

A clergyman, like any other groom, is married in the church of his bride by her own clergyman. If she belongs to the church he serves, then they may be married there by some other clergyman of his faith—his superior, a friend, or a clergyman from a neighboring parish or congregation. Occasionally, if he has an assistant, the couple is married by him. However, it is usual for a minister of his own rank or higher to perform the ceremony.

A clergyman may announce his forthcoming marriage from the pulpit on a Sunday, and invite the congregation to attend if the marriage is to take place in his house of worship. Such a procedure, though it is followed occasionally, risks the exclusion of members who did not attend services on the day the announcement was made. The sending of individual invitations, using the entire church mailing list, or an invitation in the church paper, which is sent to all the parish families, are more correct and effective procedures. When the bride comes from a distance to be married in her husband's church, the people of the congregation might give the reception, especially if the couple's joint circumstances are modest.

A minister is usually given the honor of conducting the ceremony for his own son in the bride's place of worship, with the bride's clergyman assisting. The clergyman's congregation does not usually expect to be invited en masse if the distance for the wedding is great, though various officers of the congregation might well be included in the invitation list.

When the daughter of a clergyman marries, she may be escorted to the altar by her father, with a pastor friend conducting the service until after the point where the father "gives the bride away"; then the father may conduct the remainder of the service. An alternative is for the bride to be escorted by an older brother, a brother-in-law, an uncle, or a family friend; after accompanying her to the altar, the escort may give her away, or he may take a place in a pew on the bride's side while the bride's father steps forward to give her away.

WEDDING ANNIVERSARIES

First—paper	Thirteenth—lace
Second—cotton	Fourteenth—ivory
Third—leather	Fifteenth—crystal
Fourth—linen (silk)	Twentieth—china
Fifth—wood	Twenty-fifth—silver
Sixth—iron	Thirtieth—pearl
Seventh—wool and copper	Thirty-fifth—coral
Eighth—bronze	Fortieth—ruby
Ninth—pottery (china)	Forty-fifth—sapphire
Tenth—tin (aluminum)	Fiftieth—gold
Eleventh—steel	Fifty-fifth—emerald
Twelfth—silk	Sixtieth—diamond

VII. Marriage Laws

There is a notable and regrettable lack of uniformity from state to state in marriage laws.

For the minister who serves in several states, it is difficult, nevertheless important, to keep up with the amazing variety of statutes regulating marriage.

There are variations regarding persons who are permitted to marry, the information required on the application license, the period of advance notice, and almost every facet of procedure and requirement.

Since the minister is sought out for early counsel, and stands as a "guard" at the marriage "doors," the present chapter includes some of the pertinent information regarding general marriage laws.

WHO MAY LEGALLY OFFICIATE AT A WEDDING?

Nearly all states permit either civil or religious authorities to solemnize marriages. Only one state, Maryland, restricts the right to religious officiants only.

Among the civil officers authorized to solemnize marriage, the justices of the peace are the ones who most commonly perform marriages, although governors, mayors, judges, and, in some places, notary publics, may officiate.

About three-fourths of all marriages in the United States are performed by religious officiants, because most people consider marriage a sacred undertaking. Also, the civil ceremony frequently is devoid of reverence, beauty, and dignity.

Upon moving to a new state, it is well for the minister to visit the county clerk, to familiarize himself with all the laws in question. If it is necessary to register, he should do so immediately, declaring his credentials.

It is required that a clergyman be registered either in the county clerk's office where he serves or in some county of the state.

Any lawyer could assist in answering legal questions that occur.

IS A BLOOD TEST REQUIRED?

In most states, a Wasserman or other standard laboratory blood test is required of persons planning to marry, showing freedom from venereal disease. The test can be given by a licensed physician within forty days before marriage, with the laboratory work done by the state department of health or a laboratory approved by it.

A medical certificate is presented when application for license is made. In most instances, then, a waiting period is required before the license is actually issued. The most common period of time specified is 5 days. However, this, too, varies with states.

Under certain circumstances that satisfy the court, the required advance notice can be reduced or entirely waived.

The purpose of the advance notice is to prevent hasty, fraudulent, freak, drunken, or runaway marriages that cannot stand the light of public exposure. Seldom is it a hardship for normal people to let their intentions be known several days in advance.

THE LICENSE

The law prohibits any officiant from marrying persons who have no license. Penalties may result for the one who illegally joins couples that have no license.

The license is the keystone to the whole structure of marriage regulation by the state, for it is supposed to be the proof that the applicants have met all state requirements as to age, parental consent, dissolution of previous marriage, and physical and mental capacity, and have official sanction to wed.

In most states only one person need apply for the license, a few require both parties to appear, and in a few cases it is even possible for a third party to make the application. Some states require only the statement of one or both applicants that all the requirements have been met; others require one or both to give such testimony under oath; and a few require also the affidavit of a third party.

The officiant should promptly refuse to officiate if there is the slightest evidence of irregularity, or until such can be cleared to his satisfaction.

It is extremely important that the marriage license, signed by the officiant and witnesses (two required in most states), be returned to the issuing office, for it constitutes a permanent record. The officiant is responsible for making the return, and usually there is a penalty if the delay is beyond a certain length of time—*i.e.*, 3 days in many states.

WHAT ARE THE BOUNDARIES? WHERE MUST THE WEDDING BE HELD?

In most states, the marriage must be performed in the county of the office issuing the license. In all states, it must be performed within the state where the license is issued. If a marriage is legal in the state where it is performed, it is legal everywhere, except when it is void by express statutes forbidding such marriages—*i.e.,* different races, etc. This is true of marriages in other countries as well, except when there is conflict with our marriage statutes, or when the persons are not legally free to marry.

WHAT ARE THE LEGAL AGES FOR MARRIAGE— WITH OR WITHOUT CONSENT?

The most common minimum legal age for girls to marry with parental consent is 16; without parental consent it is 18. For boys, the legal age is 18 with parental consent, and 21 without.

However, the age requirements do vary slightly from state to state, as indicated later in this chapter.

WHAT ARE THE LAWS REGARDING MARRYING RELATIVES

In all states, marriage is prohibited between sister and brother, mother and son, father and daughter, grandmother and grandson, grandfather and granddaughter, uncle and niece, aunt and nephew.

For the marrying of other relatives, there is no legal uniformity. In twenty-nine jurisdictions, first cousins may not marry. Nine states prohibit marriage to a grandniece (or grandnephew), and six states forbid marriage to a first cousin once removed. Many states also extend prohibitions to relatives by half blood (half brothers and sisters, half cousins, etc.).

Also, there are marriage prohibitions between persons who, though not related by blood, have a close affinity by marriage. The most common such prohibition (in twenty-three states) is that against marriage between stepparents and stepchildren. Twenty states forbid the marriage of father and daughter-in-law or of mother and son-in-law; eighteen prohibit a man from marrying his wife's granddaughter, even though sprung from a previous marriage; twelve will not allow a man to marry his wife's mother, or a woman her husband's father.

IS RACIAL INTERMARRIAGE LEGAL?

Almost all states forbid marriage between certain racial groups. The pairing most widely tabooed is white and Negro; however, laws in some states cover white and American Indian, white and Orientals (see the section on state marriage laws).

WHAT OTHER CONDITIONS PROHIBIT MARRIAGE?

All of the states have laws related to the marriage of the insane, feeble-minded, and mentally incapable, which are to a considerable extent inheritable. Not all states positively forbid such marriages however. Seventeen states prohibit the marriage of epileptics, seven of them making exceptions in cases where the woman involved is over 45 years of age. Two states permit hereditary epileptics to marry after they have been sterilized by an operation.

Three states prohibit the marriage of persons having infectious tuberculosis, and two forbid a person having any communicable disease to marry. Twenty-six states forbid marriages where either party has syphilis or gonorrhea.

IS COMMON-LAW MARRIAGE LEGAL?

When a man and woman make an agreement that they are husband and wife, live together in this relationship, and represent it as a marriage before their friends and the public in general, they are parties to common-law marriage. In most states, such receives no valid recognition by the law. The states that do recognize common-law marriages as legal are: Alabama, California (if entered into prior to 1895). Colorado, District of Columbia, Florida, Georgia, Idaho, Indiana, Michigan (if entered into prior to January

1957), Minnesota (if entered into prior to April 26, 1941), Mississippi (if entered into prior to 1956), Missouri (if entered into prior to March 31, 1921), Montana, Nebraska (if entered into prior to 1923), New Jersey (if entered into prior to November 30, 1939), New York (if entered into prior to April 29, 1933), Ohio, Oklahoma, Pennsylvania, Rhode Island, South Carolina, South Dakota, and Texas.

WHEN CAN A MARRIAGE BE ANNULLED?

Divorce terminates marriages that have been legally recognized, whereas annulment is a judicial declaration that no valid marriage ever existed between the parties in question. All of the states provide for annulment, the most common grounds being: not of age, mental incapacity, force or duress, consanguinity or affinity, miscegenation, and fraud of some kind, such as concealment of insanity, impotency, conviction of a felony, and prior undissolved marriage.

The average duration of marriages ending in annulment is very short (one-third last less than one year).

WHAT ARE THE MARRIAGE LAWS, BY STATES?[1, 2, 3, 4]

Alabama

Minimum ages with parental consent: men 17, women 14; without consent: men 21, women 18. Bond is required if male is under 21, female under 18. Blood test mandatory. No waiting time either before or after license. $2.00 license secured from probate judge of county in which prospective bride lives or where ceremony is to be conducted. Whites may not marry Negroes. They are permitted to marry American Indians and Orientals. First cousins, first cousins once removed, and second cousins are permitted to marry. Alabama law prohibits a man marrying his daughter, son's widow, mother, stepdaughter, stepmother, granddaughter, wife's granddaughter, sister, half sister, aunt, niece, or half niece.

Alaska

Minimum ages with parental consent: men 18, women 16; without consent: men 21, women 18. Three-day waiting period for license, none after license is issued. License fee, $2.50. Blood test mandatory. Marriage between Negroes, Orientals, and American Indians is permitted. First cousins may marry; first cousins once removed and second cousins are prohibited to marry.

Arizona

Minimum ages with parental consent: men 18, women 16; without consent: men 21, women 18. Waiting time, 48 hours from time blood test is taken. Blood test mandatory. $2.00 license secured from clerk of superior court in county where either prospective bride or groom lives, or where ceremony is to be conducted. Marriage between whites and Negroes and whites and Orientals prohibited; between whites and American Indians is permitted. Marriage of first cousins prohibited, but marriage of first cousins once removed and second cousins is permitted. Arizona law prohibits a man marrying his daughter, mother, granddaughter, grandmother, sister, half sister, aunt, or niece.

Arkansas

Minimum ages with parental consent: men 18, women 16; without consent: men 21, women 18. Blood test mandatory. Three-day waiting period for license, none after license is issued. $3.00 license secured from clerk of any county court in the state. Minister must secure from a county clerk within the state a certificate authorizing to perform marriages. Whites may not marry Negroes. However, marriage of whites and American Indians or Orientals is permitted. Marriage of first cousins is prohibited; marriage of first cousins once removed and second cousins, permitted. Arkansas law prohibits a man marrying his daughter, mother, granddaughter, grandmother, sister, half sister, aunt, or niece.

California

Minimum ages with parental consent: men 18, women 16; without consent: men 21, women 18. Blood test mandatory. No waiting period for license, either before or after issuance. $2.00 license secured from county clerk in county where ceremony is to be conducted. Blood test mandatory within 30 days of ceremony. One witness of marriage required. Imbeciles, insane, drunkards, and narcotics addicts may not marry. Marriage between whites and Negroes, Orientals, and American Indians is permitted. First cousins, first cousins once removed, and second cousins may marry. California law prohibits a man marrying his daughter, mother, granddaughter, grandmother, sister, aunt, or niece.

Colorado

Minimum ages with parental consent: men 16, women 16; without consent: men 21, women 18. Blood test mandatory. No waiting period for license, either before or after issuance. $2.00 license secured from any county clerk. Whites may marry Orientals or Indians, but not Negroes. Marriage with first cousins, first cousins once removed, and second cousins is permitted. Colorado law prohibits a man marrying his daughter, mother, granddaughter, grandmother, sister, half sister, aunt, niece or half niece.

Connecticut

Minimum ages with parental consent: men 16, women 16; without consent: men 21, women 21. Blood test mandatory. Waiting period for license, 4 days; none after license issuance. $2.00 license secured from registrar of marriages in city where ceremony is to be conducted.

Epileptics and feeble-minded may not marry. Marriage of first cousins, first cousins once removed, and second cousins is permitted. Connecticut law prohibits a man marrying his daughter, mother, granddaughter, grandmother, stepdaughter, stepmother, sister, aunt, or niece.

Delaware

Minimum ages with parental consent: men 18, women 16; without consent: men 21, women 18. Blood test mandatory. Waiting period for license, none; after license, 24 hours if one or both parties resident of state, 96 hours if both parties are not residents. $3.00 license secured from local magistrate or county clerk of peace. Minors, divorcees, patients or former patients of insane asylums, or persons on parole must secure licenses from clerks of peace or their deputies. Two witnesses of wedding are necessary. Marriage between whites and Negroes is prohibited; between whites and Orientals or American Indians, permitted. Epileptics, venereals, drunkards, insane, narcotics addicts, or those suffering from a communicable disease may not marry. Marriage of first cousins is prohibited; marriage with first cousins once removed and second cousins, permitted. Delaware law prohibits a man marrying his daughter, mother, granddaughter, grandmother, sister, aunt, or niece.

District of Columbia

Minimum ages with parental consent: men 18, women 16; without consent: men 21, women 18. No mandatory blood test. Waiting period for license, 4 days; none after license is issued. 50¢ application fee for license, and $2.00 when license is secured from the clerk of the Supreme Court of the District of Columbia. Marriage of first cousins, first cousins once removed, and second cousins is permitted. No marriage of idiots or lunatics. District of Columbia law prohibits a man marrying his daughter, mother, stepmother, granddaughter, grandmother, wife's granddaughter, wife's grandmother, sister, or aunt.

Florida
Minimum ages with parental consent: men 18, women 16; without consent: men 21, women 21. Blood test mandatory. Waiting period for license, 3 days; none after license is issued. $3.00 license secured from judge of county where prospective bride lives. Marriage of whites with Orientals and American Indians is permitted. Marriage with first cousins, first cousins once removed, and second cousins is permitted. Whites may not marry anyone with one-eighth or more Negro blood. Florida law prohibits a man marrying his daughter, mother, granddaughter, grandmother, sister, aunt, or niece.

Georgia
Minimum ages with parental consent: men 17, women 14; without consent: men 21, women 18. Blood test mandatory. No waiting period required before or after issuance of license, except 5 days if either party is younger than 21. $5.00 license secured from county clerk where prospective bride lives. If woman is out-of-state resident, license secured from clerk of county where ceremony is to be conducted. Whites cannot marry Negroes, Orientals, or American Indians. Marriage with first cousins, first cousins once removed, and second cousins is permitted. Negro ministers may conduct ceremony only for Negro couples. Georgia law prohibits a man marrying his daughter, daughter-in-law, mother-in-law, mother, stepdaughter, stepmother, granddaughter, wife's granddaughter, grandmother, sister, aunt, or niece.

Hawaii
Minimum ages with parental consent: men 18, women 16; without consent: men 20, women 20. Blood test man-

datory. Waiting period for license, 3 days; none after license is issued. License fee, $5.00. No racial restrictions.

Idaho
Minimum ages with parental consent: men 15, women 15; without consent: men 18, women 18. Blood test mandatory. No waiting period either before or after license is issued. $3.00 license secured from county recorder of any county. Marriage between whites and Negroes or Orientals is prohibited; between whites and American Indians is permitted. Marriage with first cousins is prohibited; with first cousins once removed and second cousins is permitted. Idaho law prohibits a man marrying his daughter, mother, granddaughter, grandmother, sister, half sister, aunt, or niece.

Illinois
Minimum ages with parental consent: men 18, women 16; without consent: men 21, women 18. Blood test mandatory. Waiting time for license from time blood test is taken, 1 day; none after license is issued. $3.00 license fee (except Cook County, $5.00) secured from county clerk of county where ceremony is to be conducted. Members of Society of Friends are exempt from the necessity of license. Marriage of whites with Negroes, Orientals, and American Indians is permitted. Marriage with first cousins, prohibited; with first cousins once removed and second cousins, permitted. Marriage of insane or idiots is not permitted. Illinois law prohibits a man marrying his daughter, mother, granddaughter, grandmother, sister, half sister, aunt, niece, grandaunt, or great-grandaunt.

Indiana
Minimum ages with parental consent: men 18, women 16; without consent: men 21, women 18. Blood test mandatory. Waiting period for license, 3 days; none after license issuance. $5.00 license secured from clerk of circuit

court of county where prospective bride lives. License not required for members of Society of Friends. Whites may not marry anyone with one-eighth or more Negro blood. Marriage of whites with Orientals and American Indians is permitted. Marriage with first cousins and first cousins once removed is prohibited. Marriage with second cousins is permitted. Imbeciles, epileptics, insane, narcotics addicts, drunkards, or those suffering from a communicable disease may not marry. Indiana law prohibits a man marrying his daughter, mother, granddaughter, grandmother, sister, aunt, niece, grandaunt, great-grandaunt, grandniece, or great-grandniece.

Iowa

Minimum ages with parental consent: men 18, women 16; without consent: men 21, women 18. Blood test mandatory. Waiting period for license, 3 days; none after license issuance. $3.00 license secured from clerk of district court of county where ceremony is to be conducted. There are no racial restrictions. Imbeciles, insane, or epileptics may not marry. Marriage of first cousins is prohibited. Marriage with first cousins once removed or second cousins is permitted. Iowa law prohibits a man marrying his daughter, mother, daughter-in-law, mother-in-law, stepdaughter, stepmother, granddaughter, grandmother, grandson's widow, sister, aunt, or niece.

Kansas

Minimum ages with parental consent: men 18, women 16; without consent: men 21, women 18. Blood test mandatory. Waiting period for license, 3 days; none after license issuance. $3.50 license (including $1.00 registration fee) secured from probate judge of any county. License not required for members of Society of Friends. No racial restrictions. Marriage with first cousins is prohibited; marriage with first cousins once removed or second cousins is permitted. Epileptics, feeble-minded, and insane may not marry unless the woman is over 45. Kansas law prohibits a man marrying his daughter, mother, granddaughter, grandmother, sister, half sister, aunt, or niece.

Kentucky

Minimum ages with parental consent: men 18, women 16; without consent: men 21, women 21. Blood test mandatory. Waiting period for license, 3 days; none after license issuance. $6.00 license secured from clerk of county where prospective bride lives. Marriage of whites with Negroes is prohibited; of whites with Orientals or American Indians is permitted. Marriage with first cousins and first cousins once removed is prohibited; with second cousins, permitted. Idiots or insane may not marry. Kentucky law prohibits a man marrying his daughter, mother, stepdaughter, stepmother, daughter-in-law, mother-in-law, granddaughter, grandmother, grandson's wife, wife's granddaughter, grandfather's wife, wife's grandmother, sister, aunt, niece, or grandniece, even though these relationships be dissolved by death or divorce.

Louisiana

Minimum ages with parental consent: men 18, women 16; without consent: men 21, women 21. Blood test mandatory. No waiting period for license; 72 hours after license is issued. $2.00 license secured from clerk of county court; in New Orleans from the Board of Health and judges of city courts. Three witnesses of wedding are required. Whites may not marry Negroes; marriage of whites with Orientals or American Indians is permitted. Marriage of first cousins, prohibited; with first cousins once removed or second cousins, permitted. Louisiana law prohibits a man marrying his daughter, mother, granddaughter, grandmother, sister, half sister, aunt, or niece.

Maine

Minimum ages with parental consent: men 16, women 16; without consent: men 21, women 18. Blood test mandatory. An "intention to marry" certificate must be filed with city clerk in city where ceremony is to be conducted, or in city where one of party lives, at least 5 days before the $2.00 license is issued. No waiting period is required after license issuance. Minister must secure from the secretary of state a certificate authorizing him to officiate. Two witnesses of wedding are required. There are no racial restrictions. Insane, idiots, feeble-minded, and those suffering from a communicable disease may not marry. Maine's laws prohibit a man marrying his daughter, mother, stepdaughter, stepmother, son's wife, wife's mother, granddaughter, wife's granddaughter, grandmother, wife's grandmother, grandson's wife, grandfather's wife, sister, aunt, or niece. Marriage with first cousins, first cousins once removed, or second cousins is permitted.

Maryland

Minimum ages with parental consent: men 18, women 16; without consent: men 21, women 18. Blood test is not mandatory. Waiting period for license, 48 hours; after license issuance, none. $3.00 to $6.00 license (fee depending upon county) secured from clerk of circuit court in county where marriage is to be conducted. Necessity of license is not required for members of Society of Friends. Civil marriages are prohibited. Marriage of whites with Negroes or Orientals is prohibited; with American Indians, permitted. Maryland law prohibits a man marrying his daughter, mother, daughter-in-law, mother-in-law, stepdaughter, stepmother, granddaughter, grandmother, wife's granddaughter, wife's grandmother, grandson's wife, grandfather's wife, sister, aunt, or niece. Marriage with first cousins, first cousins once removed, or second cousins is permitted.

Massachusetts

Minimum ages with parental consent: men 18, women 16; without consent: men 21, women 18. Blood test mandatory. An "intention to marry" certificate must be filed with clerk or registrar of town where party resides, or if nonresident in town where ceremony is to be conducted, at least 3 days before the $2.00 license is issued. There is no waiting period following license issuance. No marriage is allowed between insane persons incapable of contracting marriage. Marriage with first cousins, first cousins once removed, and second cousins is permitted. There are no racial prohibitions. Massacusetts law prohibits a man marrying his daughter, mother, daughter-in-law, mother-in-law, stepdaughter, stepmother, granddaughter, grandmother, wife's granddaughter, wife's grandmother, grandfather's wife, sister, aunt, or niece, even though the relationship be dissolved by death or divorce.

Michigan

Minimum ages with parental consent: men 18, women 16; without consent: men 18, women 18. Blood test mandatory. Waiting period for license, 3 days; none after license is issued. $2.00 license secured from county clerk of county where either prospective bride or groom lives; if nonresident, in county where ceremony is to be conducted. There are no racial prohibitions. Two witnesses at wedding are required. Venereals, idiots, epileptics, and insane may not marry. Marriage with first cousins is prohibited; with first cousins once removed or second cousins, permitted. Michigan law prohibits a man marrying his daughter, mother, daughter-in-law, mother-in-law, stepdaughter, stepmother, granddaughter, grandmother, wife's granddaughter, wife's grandmother, grandson's wife, grandfather's wife, sister, aunt, or niece.

Minnesota

Minimum ages with parental consent: men 18, women 16; without consent: men 21, women 18. Blood test not mandatory. Five-day waiting period for license; none after license is issued. $5.00 license secured from clerk of district court of county in which bride lives; if nonresident, from clerk of county where ceremony is to be conducted. Minister must secure from clerk of district court in same county in state a certificate authorizing him to officiate. Two witnesses at wedding are required. There are no racial prohibitions. Epileptics, idiots, insane, or feeble-minded may not marry. Marriage with first cousins or first cousins once removed is prohibited; with second cousins, permitted. Minnesota law prohibits a man marrying his daughter, mother, granddaughter, grandmother, sister, aunt, niece, grandaunt, great-grandaunt, grandniece, or great-grandniece.

Mississippi

Minimum ages with parental consent: men 17, women 15; without consent: men 21, women 21. Blood test mandatory. Three-day waiting period for license; none after license is issued. $3.00 license secured from clerk of circuit court in county where prospective bride lives. Marriage of whites and Negroes or Orientals is prohibited; whites with American Indians, permitted. Marriage with first cousins is prohibited; with first cousins once removed or second cousins, permitted. Insane and idiots may not marry. Mississippi law prohibits a man marrying his daughter, mother, stepdaughter, stepmother, sister, half sister, granddaughter, grandmother, son's widow, wife's granddaughter, aunt, or niece.

Missouri

Minimum ages with parental consent: men 15, women 15; without consent: men 21, women 18. Blood test mandatory. Three-day waiting period for license; none after license is issued. $2.55 license secured from county recorder or recorder of the city of St. Louis. Marriage of whites with Negroes or Orientals is prohibited; whites with American Indians, permitted. Marriage with first cousins is prohibited; with first cousins once removed or second cousins, permitted. Insane, imbeciles, feeble-minded, or epileptics may not marry. Missouri law prohibits a man marrying his daughter, mother, granddaughter, grandmother, sister, half sister, aunt, or niece.

Montana

Minimum ages with parental consent: men 18, women 16; without consent: men 21, women 18. Blood test mandatory. Five-day waiting period for license; none after license is issued. Marriage of whites with Negroes or Orientals is prohibited; whites with American Indians, permitted. Marriage with first cousins is prohibited; with first cousins once removed or second cousins, permitted. Montana law prohibits a man marrying his daughter, mother, sister, half sister, granddaughter, grandmother, aunt, or niece.

Nebraska

Minimum ages with parental consent: men 18, women 16; without consent: men 21, women 18. Blood test mandatory. Waiting period for license, none; after license issued, none. $5.00 license secured from clerk of any county in the state. Ministerial license is necessary. Two witnesses at wedding are required. Marriage of whites with Negroes or Orientals is prohibited; whites with American Indians, permitted. Marriage with first cousins or first cousins once removed is prohibited; with second cousins, permitted. Nebraska law prohibits a man marrying his daughter, mother, granddaughter, grandmother, sister, aunt, niece, grandaunt, or great-grandaunt.

Nevada

Minimum ages with parental consent: men 18, women 16; without consent: men 21, women 18. Blood test is not mandatory. No waiting period is required before or after obtaining license. $5.00 license secured from clerk of any county in the state. Minister must secure certificate authorizing him to officiate. Two witnesses of wedding are required. Marriage of whites with Negroes or Orientals is prohibited; whites with American Indians, permitted. Venereals, insane, and idiots may not marry. Marriage of first cousins and first cousins once removed is prohibited; marriage with second cousins is permitted. Nevada law prohibits a man marrying his daughter, mother, granddaughter, grandmother, sister, aunt, grandaunt, niece, or great-grandaunt.

New Hampshire

Minimum ages with both parental and court's consent: men 14, women 13; without consent: men 20, women 18. Blood test mandatory. An "intention to marry" certificate must be filed with clerk of town in which either party resides, or, if nonresident, with clerk of county in which ceremony is to be conducted, at least 5 days before the $3.00 license is issued. No waiting period is required after license is issued. Epileptics, imbeciles, feeble-minded, idiots, and insane may not marry. No racial restrictions. Marriage with first cousins is prohibited; with first cousins once removed or second cousins, permitted. New Hampshire law prohibits a man marrying his daughter, father's widow, son's widow, granddaughter, grandson's widow, stepdaughter, mother-in-law, sister, aunt, or niece.

New Jersey

Minimum ages with parental consent: men 18, women 16; without consent: men 21, women 18. Blood test mandatory. Waiting period for license, 72 hours; none after license is issued. $3.00 license secured from clerk of city, registrar of vital statistics, or tax assessor in the municipality where prospective bride lives; if she is a nonresident, where prospective groom lives; if both are nonresidents, in the municipality where ceremony is to be conducted. Two witnesses of wedding are required. There are no racial prohibitions. Venereals, imbeciles, insane, epileptics, and narcotics addicts may not marry. Marriage with first cousins, first cousins once removed, and second cousins is permitted. New Jersey law prohibits a man marrying his daughter, mother, granddaughter, grandmother, sister, half sister, aunt, or niece.

New Mexico

Minimum ages with parental consent: men 18, women 16; without consent: men 21, women 18. Blood test mandatory. No waiting period before or after license is issued. $5.00 license secured from county clerk of county where ceremony is to be conducted. Marriage with cousins is permitted. Two witnesses of wedding are required. There are no racial prohibitions. New Mexico law prohibits a man marrying his daughter, mother, granddaughter, grandmother, sister, half sister, aunt, or niece.

New York

Minimum ages with parental consent: men 16, women 14; without consent: men 21, women 18. Blood test mandatory. No waiting period to obtain license; 24 hours after license is issued. Marriage may not be solemnized within 3 days from date of blood test. $4.00 license secured from clerk of city in which prospective bride lives; if nonresident, in city where ceremony is to be conducted. In New York City, it is essential for clergyman to register with city clerk. One witness of ceremony besides officiant is required. There are no racial prohibitions. Idiots, insane, and venereals may not marry. Marriage with first cousins, first cousins once removed, and second cousins is permitted. New York law prohibits a man marrying his daughter, mother, granddaughter, grandmother, sister, half sister, niece, or aunt.

North Carolina

Minimum ages with parental consent: men 16, women 16; without consent: men 18, women 18. Blood test mandatory. No waiting period either before or after license is issued. $5.00 license secured from registrar of deeds of county where ceremony is to be conducted. One or more witnesses required. Marriage of whites with Negroes or American Indians is prohibited; of whites with Orientals, permitted. Venereals, idiots, imbeciles, and those afflicted with infectious tuberculosis may not marry. Insane persons may marry only after eugenic sterilization. Marriage with first cousins or first cousins once removed is prohibited; with second cousins, permitted. North Carolina law prohibits a man marrying his daughter, mother, sister, grandmother, aunt, or niece.

North Dakota

Minimum ages with parental consent: men 18, women 15; without consent: men 21, women 18. Blood test mandatory. No waiting period before or after license is issued. $1.00 license secured from judge of county where either party lives, or county to which an unorganized area is attached for judicial purposes. License is not granted to nonresidents. Marriage of whites with Negroes is prohibited; marriage of whites with Orientals or American Indians, permitted. Marriage with first cousins is prohibited; with first cousins once removed or second cousins, permitted. Marriage is prohibited for imbeciles, criminals, drunkards, idiots, feeble-minded, and insane, except when the woman is over 45. North Dakota law prohibits a man marrying his daughter, mother, granddaughter, grandmother, sister, half sister, niece, or aunt.

Ohio

Minimum ages with parental consent: men 18, women 16; without consent: men 21, women 21. Blood test mandatory. Five-day waiting period for license; none after license is issued. $2.15 license secured from probate judge of county where prospective bride lives; no license issued to nonresidents. Before officiating at a ceremony, the minister must obtain a license from probate judge of the county. There are no racial prohibitions. Habitual drunkards, epileptics, narcotics addicts, imbeciles, and insane may not marry. Marriage with first cousins, first cousins once removed, or second cousins is prohibited. Ohio law prohibits a man marrying his daughter, mother, granddaughter, grandmother, sister, niece, aunt, grandaunt, great-grandaunt, or great-grandniece.

Oklahoma

Minimum ages with parental consent: men 18, women 15; without consent: men 21, women 18. Blood test mandatory. No waiting period for obtaining license, unless couple is underage—then 3 days are required. $5.00 license secured from judge or clerk of county where ceremony is to be conducted. Two witnesses of wedding are required. Minister must file his credentials with some county judge of the state. Marriage of Negroes with other races is prohibited; whites may marry Orientals or American Indians. Marriage with first cousins, first cousins once removed, or second cousins is prohibited. Oklahoma law prohibits a man marrying his daughter, mother, stepdaughter, stepmother, sister, half-sister, granddaughter, grandmother, aunt, or niece.

Oregon

Minimum ages with parental consent: men 18, women 15; without consent: men 21, women 18. Blood test mandatory. $3.00 license secured from clerk of any county. Minister must file credentials with county clerk. Two witnesses of wedding are required. There are no racial prohibitions. Marriage with first cousins is prohibited;

with first cousins once removed or second cousins, permitted. Oregon law prohibits a man marrying his daughter, mother, sister, half sister, grandmother, granddaughter, aunt, half aunt, niece, or half niece.

Pennsylvania

Minimum ages with parental consent: men 16, women 16; without consent: men 21, women 21. Blood test mandatory. Three-day waiting period for license; none after license is issued. $3.00 license secured from clerk of orphan's court of county in which either lives or where ceremony is to be conducted. Imbeciles, epileptics, persons of unsound mind, and persons under the influence of intoxicating liquor or narcotics may not marry. There are no racial prohibitions. Marriage with first cousins is prohibited; with first cousins once removed and second cousins, permitted. Pennsylvania law prohibits a man marrying his daughter, mother, stepdaughter, stepmother, daughter-in-law, sister, granddaughter, grandmother, wife's granddaughter, aunt, or niece.

Rhode Island

Minimum ages with parental consent: men 18, women 16; without consent: men 21, women 21. Blood test mandatory. Marriage may not be solemnized within 3 days from date of blood test. No waiting period after license, unless parties are nonresidents. $2.00 license secured from clerk of city in which either lives; if they are nonresidents, in city where ceremony is to be conducted. Minister must secure license from clerk of town or city. Two witnesses of ceremony are required. There are no racial prohibitions. Lunatics may not marry. Rhode Island law prohibits a man marrying his daughter, mother, sister, stepdaughter, stepmother, daughter-in-law, mother-in-law, granddaughter, grandmother, grandson's wife, grandfather's wife, wife's granddaughter, wife's grandmother, aunt, or niece.

South Carolina

Minimum ages with parental consent: men 16, women 14; without consent: men 18, women 18. No blood test mandatory. 24-hour waiting period is required before obtaining license from time blood test is taken; no waiting period after license is issued. $4.00 license secured from judge of probate court. Marriage of whites with Negroes or American Indians is prohibited; of whites with Orientals, permitted. Marriage of idiots and lunatics is prohibited. South Carolina law prohibits a man marrying his daughter, mother, sister, stepdaughter, stepmother, son's wife, wife's mother, granddaughter, grandmother, grandfather's wife, wife's granddaughter, wife's grandmother, aunt, or niece.

South Dakota

Minimum ages with parental consent: men 18, women 16; without consent: men 21, women 18. Blood test mandatory. No waiting period required either before or after license is issued. $2.50 license secured from clerk of court of county where ceremony is to be conducted. Two witnesses of ceremony are required. Marriage of whites with Negroes or Orientals is prohibited; of whites with American Indians, permitted. Marriage with first cousins is prohibited; with first cousins once removed or second cousins, permitted. South Dakota law prohibits a man marrying his daughter, mother, sister, half sister, granddaughter, grandmother, son's wife, aunt, or niece.

Tennessee

Minimum ages with parental consent: men 16, women 16; without consent: men 21, women 21. Blood test mandatory. No waiting period except for those who are underage. Three-day waiting period is required before obtaining license; none after license is issued. $2.00 license secured from clerk of county where prospective bride lives or where ceremony is to be conducted. Written parental consent is necessary when parties are under 21. Marriage of whites with Negroes is prohibited; whites with Orientals or American Indians, permitted. Those of unsound mind are prohibited from marrying. Tennessee law prohibits a man marrying his daughter, mother, sister, half sister, stepdaughter, stepmother, granddaughter, grandmother, son's wife, grandson's wife, wife's granddaughter, niece, half niece, grandniece, half grandniece, and great-grandniece.

Texas

Minimum ages with written parental consent: men 16, women 14; without consent: men 21, women 18. Blood test mandatory. No waiting period for license unless parties are underage—then 3 days; none after license is issued. $3.00 license secured from clerk of any county. Marriage of whites with Negroes is prohibited; with Orientals or American Indians, permitted. Texas law prohibits a man marrying his daughter, mother, sister, half sister, stepdaughter, stepmother, granddaughter, wife's granddaughter, son's widow, aunt, half aunt, niece, or half niece.

Utah

Minimum ages with parental consent: men 16, women 14; without consent: men 21, women 18. Blood test mandatory. No waiting period either before or after license is issued. $2.50 license secured from clerk of county where prospective bride lives. If bride is 18 or older, or a widow, the license may be secured in any county upon written application. Two witnesses of the ceremony are required. Marriage of whites with Negroes or Orientals is prohibited; with American Indians, permitted. Marriage of first cousins is prohibited; with first cousins once removed or second cousins, permitted. Utah law prohibits a man marrying his daughter, mother, sister, half sister, granddaughter, grandmother, aunt, niece, grandaunt, or grandniece.

Vermont

Minimum ages with parental consent: men 18, women 16; without consent: men 21, women 18. Blood test mandatory. No waiting period for license; 5-day waiting period is required after license is issued. $3.00 certificate authorizing marriage secured from clerk of city where man lives; if he is nonresident, from clerk of city where woman lives; if both are nonresidents, from clerk in city where ceremony is to be conducted. There are no racial prohibitions. Those of unsound mind may not marry. Vermont law prohibits a man marrying his daughter, mother, sister, stepdaughter, stepmother, son's wife, granddaughter, grandmother, grandfather's wife, wife's granddaughter, wife's grandmother, aunt, or niece, whether the relationship is dissolved by death or by divorce.

Virginia

Minimum ages with parental consent: men 18, women 16; without consent: men 21, women 21. Blood test mandatory. No waiting period either before or after license is issued. $4.00 license secured from clerk of circuit court in county where prospective bride lives; if she is a nonresident, in county where ceremony is to be conducted. A $500 bond from circuit court is required by minister, authorizing him to perform marriage ceremonies. Whites may marry only whites. Habitual criminals, idiots, imbeciles, insane, and venereals may not marry. Virginia law prohibits a man marrying his daughter, mother, sister, half sister, stepmother, granddaughter, grandmother, wife's daughter, wife's granddaughter, son's wife, aunt, or niece, even though the relationship is dissolved by death or divorce.

Washington

Minimum ages with parental consent: men 15, women 15; without consent: men 21, women 18. Medical certificate or affidavit is required by males only. Three-day waiting period is required for license; none after license is issued. $5.00 license secured from county auditor. Two witnesses of wedding are necessary. There are no racial prohibitions. Habitual criminals, drunkards, epileptics, feeble-minded, idiots, insane, venereals, and those afflicted with advanced tuberculosis may not marry unless the woman is 45 or over. Marriage of first cousins or first cousins once removed is prohibited; with second cousins, permitted. Washington law prohibits a man marrying his daughter, mother, sister, half sister, granddaughter, grandmother, aunt, niece, half aunt, half niece, grandaunt, grandniece, great-grandaunt, and great-grandniece.

West Virginia

Minimum ages with parental consent: men 18, women 16; without consent: men 21, women 21. Blood test mandatory. Three-day waiting period before obtaining license; none after license is issued. $2.00 license secured from clerk of county court of county where prospective bride lives. $1,500 bond and filing of credentials with circuit or county clerk are required by minister before conducting wedding ceremonies. Marriage of whites with Negroes is prohibited; with Orientals or American Indians, permitted. Marriage of first cousins, first cousins once removed, or second cousins is prohibited. West Virginia law prohibits a man marrying his daughter, mother, sister, half sister, stepdaughter, stepmother, granddaughter, grandmother, wife's granddaughter, wife's grandmother, daughter-in-law, aunt, niece, or wife of nephew, whether or not the relationship is dissolved by divorce or death.

Wisconsin

Minimum ages with parental consent: men 18, women 16; without consent: men 21, women 18. Blood test mandatory. Five-day waiting period before obtaining license; none after license is issued. $1.50 license secured from clerk of county where either party lives; if they are nonresidents, in county where ceremony is to be conducted. A certificate authorizing the minister to perform marriage ceremonies must be secured fom the clerk of the circuit court. Two witnesses of the ceremony are required. There are no racial prohibitions. Marriage with first cousins is prohibited, unless the woman is older than 50; with first cousins once removed, prohibited; with second cousins, permitted. Idiots, insane, epileptics, or feeble-minded may not marry. Wisconsin law prohibits a man marrying his daughter, mother, sister, granddaughter, grandmother, aunt, niece, grandaunt grandniece, great-grandaunt, and great-grandniece.

Wyoming

Minimum ages with parental consent: men 18, women 16; without consent: men 21, women 21. Blood test mandatory. No waiting period is required either before or after license is issued. $2.00 license secured from clerk of county where ceremony is to be conducted. Two witnesses of the ceremony are required. Marriage of whites with Negroes or Orientals is prohibited; with American Indians, permitted. Marriage of first cousins is prohibited; with first cousins once removed or second cousins, permitted. Wyoming law prohibits a man marrying his daughter, mother, sister, half sister, granddaughter, grandmother, aunt, or niece.

State Laws of Divorce

State	Adultery	Cruelty	Desertion	Nonsupport	Alcoholism	Felony	Impotency	Pregnancy At Marriage	Drug Addiction	Fraudulent Contract	Other Causes	Residence Time	Time Between Interlocutory and Final Decrees
Alabama	x	x	x	x	x	x	x	x	x		A-Q-K-W	1 Year*	None-R
Alaska	x	x	x	x	x	x	x		x		F-K	1 Year	None
Arizona	x	x	x	x	x	x	x	x			B-X	1 Year	None-S
Arkansas	x	x	x	x	x	x	x				B-Y-K	3 Months*	None
California	x	x	x	x	x	x					K	1 Year	1 Year
Colorado	x	x	x	x	x	x	x		x		K-W	1 Year*	None
Connecticut	x	x	x	x	x	x				x	K	3 Years	None
Delaware	x	x	x	x							K-Y-P	2 Years*	3 Months
District of Columbia	x		x								X-Z	1 Year	10 Days
Florida	x	x	x	x	x	x	x		x		A	6 Months	None
Georgia	x	x	x	x	x	x	x	x	x	x	K	6 Months	**-U
Hawaii	x	x	x	x	x	x	x				K-†	2 Years	S
Idaho	x	x	x	x	x	x	x		x		X-K	6 Weeks	None
Illinois¹	x	x	x		x	x	x				A-C	1 Year*	None
Indiana	x	x	x	x	x	x	x				K	1 Year	None
Iowa	x	x	x	x	x	x		x				1 Year	None-S
Kansas	x	x	x	x	x	x	x	x		x	K	1 Year*	None-T
Kentucky	x	x	x	x	x	x	x			x	C-D-E-X-K	1 Year	None
Louisiana	x					x					X-Z	1 Year*	None
Maine	x	x	x	x	x		x		x			6 Months	None
Maryland	x	x	x			x	x	x			Y-K	1 Year*	None
Massachusetts	x	x	x	x	x	x	x		x			5 Years*	6 Mo.-L

State									Code	Period	Note
Michigan	x	x	x	x	x	x	x			1 Year	None
Minnesota	x	x	x		x	x	x		K-W	1 Year	None-T
Mississippi	x	x	x		x	x	x		K	1 Year*	None-U
Missouri	x	x	x	x	x		x		B-J	1 Year	None
Montana	x	x	x	x	x	x	x		K	1 Year	None
Nebraska	x	x	x	x	x	x	x		K	2 Years*	6 Months
Nevada	x	x	x	x	x	x	x		Y-K	6 Weeks	None
New Hampshire	x	x	x	x	x	x	x		D	1 Year*	None
New Jersey	x	x	x		x	x				2 Years*	3 Months
New Mexico	x	x	x	x	x	x	x		K-F	1 Year*	None
New York	x				x					1 Year*	3 Mo.-M*
North Carolina	x	x		x	x			x	Q-K-X	6 Months	None
North Dakota	x	x	x	x	x	x	x		K	1 Year	**-U
Ohio	x	x	x	x	x	x		x		1 Year	None.
Oklahoma	x	x	x	x	x	x		x	F-K	6 Months	6 Months
Oregon	x	x	x	x	x	x			B-K	1 Year	None-T
Pennsylvania	x	x	x	x	x	x		x	B	1 Year*	None
Rhode Island	x	x	x	x	x	x		x	H-K-X	2 Years	6 Months
South Carolina	x	x	x	x	x	x		x		1 Year	None
South Dakota	x	x	x	x	x	x			K	1 Year*	None
Tennessee	x	x	x	x	x	x			A-B	1 Year	None
Texas	x	x	x	x	x	x			K-X	1 Year	None-N
Utah	x	x	x	x	x	x			W-K	3 Months	3 Months
Vermont	x	x	x	x	x				Y-K	6 Months	6 Mo.-O*
Virginia	x	x	x	x	x	x	x		I-B	1 Year	None-V*
Washington	x	x	x	x	x	x		x	B-X-K	1 Year	None
West Virginia²	x	x	x	x	x	x				2 Years*	None-R-U
Wisconsin	x	x	x	x	x	x	x		X-W	2 Years	1 Year
Wyoming	x	x	x	x	x	x	x		B-J-K-X	60 Days*	None

SEE FOOTNOTES ON FOLLOWING PAGE.

* Exceptions are to be noted. ** Determined by court order. Georgia, period of 30 days to elapse before right to remarry. ¹Requires 60 days' notice of intention to sue. ²No minimum residence required in adultery cases. A — Violence. B — Indignities. C — Loathsome disease. D — Joining religious order disbelieving in marriage. E — Unchaste behavior after marriage. F — Incompatibility. G — Unchastity of wife prior to marriage. H — Any gross misbehavior or wickedness. I — Wife being a prostitute. J — Husband being a vagrant. K—5 years insanity. Exceptions: 18 months, Alaska; 2 years, Nevada, Washington, Wyoming; 3 years, Arkansas, California, Colorado, Georgia, Hawaii, Maryland, Mississippi, Oregon; 6 years, Idaho; 10 years, North Carolina. L — Defendant must wait 2 years to remarry. M — Plaintiff, 3 months; defendant may not marry before 3 years without consent of court. So-called Enoch Arden law provides for annulment of marriage for absence of either party for 5 successive years if unknown to be alive; void marriages, like bigamy, require no waiting time. N — Except in cruelty cases, 1 year to remarry. O — Plaintiff, 6 months; defendant, 2 years to remarry. P — If guilty spouse is sentenced to infamous punishment. Q — Crime against nature. R — 60 days to remarry. S — 1 year to remarry; Hawaii, 1 year with minor child. T — 6 months to remarry; in Kansas, 30 days. U — Adultery cases, remarriage in discretion of court. V — 4 months to remarry. W — Separation for 3 years after decree for same. In Alabama, 4 years. In Minnesota and Wisconsin, 5 years. X — Separation no cohabitation — 5 years. Exceptions: Louisiana and North Carolina, 2 years; Texas, 7 years; Rhode Island, 10 years. Y — Separation no cohabitation — 3 years. Z — Separation for 2 years after decree for same; District of Columbia and Louisiana, 1 year. † If either party has contracted Hansen's disease.

The plaintiff can invariably remarry in the same state where he or she procured a decree of divorce or annulment. Not so the defendant, who is barred, except in certain states. After a period of time has elapsed, even the offender can apply for special permission.

The U.S. Supreme Court in a 5-4 opinion, ruled April 18, 1949, that one-sided quick divorces could be challenged as illegal if notice of the action was not served on the divorced partner within the divorcing states, excepting where the partner was represented at the proceedings.

Enoch Arden Laws. Disappearance and unknown to be alive. Connecticut, 7 years absence; New Hampshire, 2 years; New York, 5 years (dissolution); Vermont, 7 years.

VIII. Wedding Prayers

O God of Abraham, God of Isaac, God of Jacob, bless this man and this woman, and sow the seeds of eternal life in their hearts, that whatsoever in Thy holy Word they shall profitably learn, they may indeed fulfill the same. Look, O Lord, mercifully on them from heaven, and bless them: as Thou didst send Thy blessings upon Abraham and Sarah to their great comfort, so vouchsafe to send Thy blessings upon this man and this woman, that they, obeying Thy will, and always being in safety under Thy protection, may abide in Thy love unto their lives' end, through Jesus Christ our Lord.

Almighty God, who at the beginning didst create our first parents, Adam and Eve, and didst sanctify and join them together in marriage, pour upon these persons the riches of Thy grace, sanctify and bless them, that they may please Thee both in body and soul, and live together in holy love unto their lives' end. Amen.

FOR REHEARSAL

Heavenly Father of us all, who hast in Thy wisdom and providence ordained marriage for the happiness and welfare of Thy children and the procreation of the race, look with favor upon this union. As this man and this woman, who have grown to love, trust, and respect one another, come to the formal and public dedication of themselves to each other in holy matrimony, grant them stability, maturity, sobriety, and reverence. Help us who share in this high experience to realize its sacredness. Give to each of us a sense of personal responsibility in our assignment, that we may honor Thee, in whose name we pray. Amen.

INVOCATION FOR WEDDING DINNERS

O Thou to whom we owe the gift of life, the provisions for our care, the capacity to love, the support of family, and the joy of friendship: we express our gratitude for the "ties that bind our hearts to Thee in Christian love," through Jesus Christ. Amen.

Our God and Father, whose nature is love, we thank Thee for this happy hour that brings us together as family and friends of ———————— and ————————. As we share in food and fellowship honoring this couple, may we be mindful of the manifestations of Thy love. Amen.

WEDDING PRAYERS

Gracious God and Father of us all, Giver of life and love, within the soul of this man and this maid Thou hast kindled the divine fire of Thine own nature. Grant that it may burn with an ever-increasing intensity until it fuses their lives into perfect oneness.

We pray Thee to make their united life pure and strong and deathless; that no dark cloud of sordidness may obscure the clear light of their devotion, and that no gray disenchantment of the years may have power to kill their dreams.

Teach them to master the high and holy art of unselfishness, that they may ever vie with each other in seeing which can give up the more, in thinking less of their rights and more of their duties; thus may they overcome the selfishness of youth in the passion of their self-surrender.

Make them wise to weigh the values of life, that they may never slay the great things for the sake of any littleness. Forbid that any tyranny of fashion or glamour of cheap fun should ever rob them of the wholesome peace and inward satisfaction which only loyalty to the best can give.

And, O God, keep them together; that most of all. May no one ever come between them—whether parent or child, or intimate friend. And, should reverses come, continually call to their remembrance that if they but keep together, no untoward circumstance shall overpower them; they shall stand unscathed and unembittered.

Grant that they build an altar in their home, dear God, a secret shrine to Thee, where daily they may talk with Thee and best learn how to live. Thus may their love outlast the fires of youth, warm old age, scorn death, and endure eternally in heaven.

In Christ's name we ask it. Amen.[1]

Our Heavenly Father, who hast willed the holy estate of marriage and who has taught us the way of love, we ask that Thou wouldst bless this union. As this home is established, may it be endowed with true devotion, spiritual commitments, and personal initiatives.

Give to this man and this woman the ability to keep the vow and covenant between them made. Where selfishness would show itself, give love; where mistrust is a temptation, give confidence; where misunderstanding intrudes, give gentleness and patience.

Give, our Father, times of joy, peace, and happiness. May this husband and wife in such moments acknowledge the source from which such privileges come. We realize, our Father, that life does not unfold without its bitter moments. Therefore we ask that Thou wouldst give to this union the patience to endure affliction. When suffering becomes their lot, give them a strong faith and an abiding hope. Should tragedy be woven into the fabric of this marriage, give them substance wherein they can comfort one another. May they not demand of Thee a reason for everything, but may doubt give way to trust. Help us to realize that Thou dost teach us in many ways.

If Thou shouldst bless this home, our Father, with children, give to this couple the qualities of true parenthood. Make this home a shelter from that which corrupts and destroys, and may it be a school wherein they may be fitted for life and service in the Kingdom of God.

Hear this prayer, we ask, petitioned through Jesus Christ our Lord. Amen.[2]

A BRIDE'S WEDDING-DAY PRAYER
(*Copy may be given to bride at rehearsal.*)

Heavenly Father, my heart is filled with rapture and gratitude for the one who seems worthy of my deepest commitment and companionship.

Today, as we are united in Holy Matrimony, I thank Thee for the teachings that have guided my life, the love which has surrounded me, the providence which directed my decisions, and my parents and friends who share this high moment.

Help me to prove to be a loving sweetheart, faithful helpmate, and congenial companion. May my voice not lose the tender tone it has known in courtship's smiling days. Grant to me, O Lord, the wisdom to make home the best loved of all places, the health to fulfill my duties cheerfully, and the grace and disposition to meet constructively the problems and irritations that will arise.

If it be Thy will, grant to me the privilege of parenthood, and the virtues of good motherhood.

When all my youthful charms have vanished, and the lines of care and age have diminished physical attraction, may we be found walking hand in hand by the bond of Thy eternal love, through Jesus Christ. Amen.

A GROOM'S WEDDING-DAY PRAYER
(*Copy may be given to groom at rehearsal.*)

My God and Father, how marvelous is thy plan for the fulfilment of personality and life. I thank Thee for the one who has grown to love me and who this day gives herself to my keeping. Together may we grow in love and affection and mutuality until two hearts beat as one.

O Lord, grant that I may be worthy of her trust, love, devotion, and surrender of name. Fill me with the Christlike spirit of thoughtfulness, unselfishness, self-control, dependability, and understanding that will make for a happy and abiding marriage. May no deeds or words of mine dim her eyes with tears of grief.

Give me the grace to accept her parents as my own, and to be worthy of their acceptance of me. If it be possible, bless our union with the gift of children, and us with the wisdom of responsible parents.

May the years together bring to full blossom the love of our hearts, faithful service in Thy Kingdom, and the glory of Thy Holy Name. Amen.

NEWLYWEDS' PRAYER
(To be used as a good-night devotional on the wedding day.)

O God, we will wonder no more that this day has been different for us from all the other days. There has been a light in the air, a glory in the sky, and a glamour on human faces, and we give Thee thanks.

We thank Thee for the people who have made the day so good; for our parents with their brave but lonely hearts and their self-forgetful service; for the companions of our youth who have shared the joy and the work of the day; for the sympathetic and gracious goodwill of the minister; and for all good wishes from sincere and loving hearts.

We give Thee thanks each for the other. Grant us some day to know fully the mystery of Thy plan by which these lives of ours have moved to seek each other out above all others to find completion for what would otherwise be imperfect living. Reveal unto us increasingly the beauty of our marriage vows.

So, our Father, we go forward seeking Thy guidance and Thy will. Hallow every hour of our united lives. Grant that our love be a holy of holies, so that we may find Thy face. Amen.[3]

WEDDING BENEDICTIONS
The Lord bless, preserve and keep you. The Lord mercifully with His favor look upon you, and fill you with all

spiritual benediction and grace, that you may so live together in this life that in the world to come you may have
life everlasting. Amen.

And now may the courage of the early morning's dawning, and the strength of the eternal hills, and the peace of
the evening's ending and the love of God be in your hearts
now and forevermore. Amen.[4]

And now may He who walked in intimate companionship
with the first human pair in the days of their innocence;
and He who coming in sorrow made the marriage feast to
rejoice by His miraculous ministry; and He who dwelling
in your hearts can make your home a habitation of love
and peace—the Father, Son and Holy Spirit—be with you
evermore. Amen.[5]

IX.   Marriage Services

A BAPTIST MARRIAGE SERVICE[1]
(Used by Dr. James Randolph Hobbs)

Holy and happy is the sacred hour when two devoted
hearts are bound by the enchanting ties of matrimony. And
these precious evidences of purity of heart and contentment
of mind, for all their future, are made more sure, when the
contracting parties enter this glad time, clad in the comely
robes of reverence, humility, and faith, that they may then
be blessed of our Heavenly Father, Maker of us all—the
One who has ordained marriage as the cornerstone of
family life and the guarantee of honorable human society.
First and noblest of human contracts, marriage was

divinely instituted when Jehovah God spoke the nuptial words to Adam and Eve in the Garden of Eden. Jesus of Nazareth honored its celebration by his presence at the wedding in Cana of Galilee, and chose its beautiful relations as the figure of that benign union between himself and his Church. Paul, militant missionary Apostle, commends it as a worthy institution, alike essential to social order, human efficiency, and well-being while the race inhabits the earth, and tells the husband to love his wife as Christ loved his Church and gave himself for it, and the wife to be faithful to her husband, even as the Church is obedient to Christ in everything. Thus the two, husband and wife, forsaking all others become one flesh, one in thought, intent, and hope, in all the concerns of the present life.

You, ———————, and you, ———————, having come to me signifying your desire to be formally united in marriage, and being assured that no legal, moral, or religious barriers hinder this proper union, I command you to join your right hands and give heed to the questions now asked you.

———————, in taking the woman whom you hold by the right hand to be your lawful and wedded wife, I require you to promise to love and cherish her, to honor and sustain her, in sickness as in health, in poverty as in wealth, in the bad that may darken your days, in the good that may light your ways, and to be true to her in all things until death alone shall part you.

Do you so promise?

———————, in taking the man who holds you by the right hand to be your lawful and wedded husband, I require you to promise to love and cherish him, to honor and sustain him, in sickness as in health, in poverty as in wealth, in the bad that may darken your days, in the good that may light your ways, and to be true to him in all things until death alone shall part you.

Do you so promise?

Then are you devoted to each other until death parts you.

The minister will take the ring from the receptacle of the ringbearer, or from the groomsman, and read the following:

From time immemorial, the ring has been used to seal important covenants. When the race was young and parliaments unknown, the great seal of State was fixed upon a ring worn by the reigning monarch, and its stamp was the sole sign of imperial authority. Friends often exchanged the simple band of gold as enduring evidence of good will, while many a hero and heroine of immortal song and thrilling tale threaded winding paths of intrigue and adventure, safe and unhurt, bearing as a magic talisman the signet of some great benefactor. From such impressive precedents the golden circlet, most prized of jewels, has come to its loftiest prestige in the symbolic significance it vouches at the hymeneal altar. Here untarnishable material and unique form become the precious tokens of the pure and abiding qualities of the ideal marital state.

The minister hands the ring to the groom, instructing him to place it upon the third finger of the bride's left hand and to hold it while the minister propounds the following questions:

Do you, _____, give this ring to _____ _____ as a token of your love for her?

The man shall answer:

I do.

Will you, _____, take this ring as a token of _____'s love for you and will you wear it as a token of your love for him?

The woman shall answer:

I will.

Where the double ring ceremony is desired, the minister will take the other ring from the receptacle of the ringbearer, or from the groomsman, and hand it to the bride, instructing her to place it upon the third finger of the groom's left hand and to hold it in place while the minister propounds the following questions:

Do you, _____, give this ring to _____
_____ as a token of your love for him?

The woman shall answer:

I do.

Will you, _____, take this ring as a token of
_____'s love for you, and will you wear it as a
token of your love for her?

The man shall answer:

I will.

*The minister will now instruct the couple to rejoin their
right hands, after which he will repeat the following:*

Having pledged your faith in, and love to, each other, and
having sealed your solemn marital vows by giving and receiving the ring (or rings), acting in the authority vested
in me by the laws of this State, and looking to Heaven for
divine sanction, I pronounce you husband and wife in the
presence of God and these assembled witnesses. Therefore,
let all men take care in the sight of God that this holy covenant shall ever remain sacred.

Prayer:

Holy, Righteous, and Merciful Father, alike Creator,
Preserver, and Redeemer of mankind, fill these thy servants
with a deep sense of the solemn obligations which they
have just assumed. Guide them to look to thee for grace
in their efforts to discharge these obligations with honor
to themselves, in thy sight and in the sight of men. Ordain
that their love now mutually plighted, may never falter
whatever course life may take with them. Crown their lives
with loving kindness and tender mercies, and provide for
their protection while they travel the uneven way that leads
from now to the end. Give them a rich measure of material
prosperity, and lead them into the fulness of spiritual understanding and holy living, that they may have an abundant
entrance into the joys everlasting. So we pray through
Jesus Christ our Lord.

The Lord bless and keep you. The Lord make his face

to shine upon you and be gracious unto you. The Lord lift up his countenance upon you and give you peace, through Jesus Christ our Lord. Amen.

A DISCIPLE'S MARRIAGE SERVICE[2]
(Used by Dr. G. Edwin Osborn)

At the day and time appointed for solemnization of matrimony, the persons to be married shall come into the body of the Church, or shall be ready in some proper house, with their friends and neighbors; and there, standing together, the man on the right hand, and the woman on the left, the minister shall say:

May God be gracious to us and bless us, and make his face to shine upon us, through Jesus Christ our Lord. Amen.

When Jesus was invited with his disciples to the marriage, he gladly accepted the invitation, and there began his ministry and his acts of power. Thus also we are now assembled, to be after him witnesses of the pledges this man and this woman are to make to each other, and to set them forth in their new estate of marriage by our prayers and Christian greetings.

Let us pray. Our eternal Father, whose very nature is love, and from whom cometh every good and perfect gift; look with thy favor upon these thy servants who desire to make their vows before thee, and to seek thy blessing upon the solemn engagement to which they now pledge themselves.

Send down upon them, we beseech thee, thy heavenly benediction; bestow upon them the gift of thy Holy Spirit, that he may sanctify their love and be himself the unity between them; keep them ever faithful to their holy covenant, and may they live together all their days in true love and perfect peace; through Jesus Christ our Lord. Amen.

Then shall the minister say:

Who gives this woman to be married to this man?

Then the father, or whoever takes his place, shall answer:
I do.

Then, speaking to the persons who are to be married, the minister shall say:

The rite of marriage in which you two come now to be united is the first and oldest rite of the world, celebrated since the beginning of the human race. Long before men had developed ceremony or inaugurated priests, marriage was celebrated, with God the creator its first priest and witness and guest. It is his institution for the comfort and convenience of mankind, and is therefore enshrined with dignity and honor for all who enter into it lawfully and in true affection.

Marriage was confirmed by Christ's solemn word, and adorned and blessed by his presence at the wedding feast in Cana of Galilee. It is set forth in the New Testament as signifying the mystical union between Christ and his Church. It is a sacrament of grace to all who enter into it under the blessing of God, and it will remain to them a bond of happiness and peace so long as his presence is kept in their hearts to sanctify the love between them.

Thus marriage will be to you, if you have it in your hearts to beautify and enrich it by your tender devotions, your mindfulness in little things, your patience and sacrifice of self to each other. All of which I charge on you here in God's sight to remember and to do, even as you will ever pray for yourselves.

To signify your willingness to engage upon these obligations, and as a seal of the holy vows you are now to make, you will join your right hands.

Then shall the minister say to the man:

Will you, ——————, take ——————, whom you hold by the hand, to be your wedded wife; promising to keep, cherish, and defend her, and to be her faithful and true husband so long as you both shall live?

The man shall answer:
I will.

Then shall the minister say to the woman:

Will, you, _____, take _____,
whom you hold by the hand, to be your wedded husband;
promising to adhere unchangeably to him in all life's
changes, and to be his loving and true wife so long as you
both shall live?

The woman shall answer:

I will.

Single-Ring Service

. . *Then shall they loose their hands, and the minister shall
say to the man:*

_____, will you seal your sacred troth by
the giving of a ring in pledge that you will faithfully perform
your vows?

The man shall answer:

I will.

*The man, receiving the ring from his groomsman, de-
livers it to the minister, who says:*

This ring is of precious metal; so let your love be the
most precious possession of your hearts. It is a circle, unbroken; so let your love each for the other be unbroken
through all your earthly days.

Then shall the minister say to the woman:

_____, as a token and a pledge that you will
faithfully perform your holy vows, will you so receive and
wear this ring?

The woman shall answer:

I will.

Then the minister addressing the man, shall say:

Forasmuch as the husband imparts to his wife his name,
and receives her into his care and keeping, I give you this
ring that you may place it on the finger of your bride as a
token, and in pledge that you so receive her.

Thus you are to compass about her life with strength and
protecting love.

Addressing the woman, the minister continues:

Thus you are to wear this ring as the enclosing bond of reverence and trust.

Addressing both the man and the woman, the minister continues:

Thus you both are to fulfill the perfect circle of duty that makes you one.

Double-Ring Service

Then shall they loose their hands, and the minister shall say to them:

Will you each seal your sacred troth by the giving of a ring in pledge that you will faithfully perform your vows?

The man and woman, each shall answer:

I will.

The man, receiving the ring from his groomsman, and the woman, from the maid of honor, deliver them to the minister, who says:

These rings are of precious metal; so let your love be the most precious possession of your hearts. Each is a circle unbroken; so let your love, one for the other, be unbroken through all your earthly days.

Then shall the minister say to the woman:

_____, as a token and a pledge that you will faithfully perform your holy vows, will you so receive and wear this ring?

The woman shall answer:

I will.

Then the minister, addressing the man, shall say:

_____, indicating your responsibility to _____ to receive her into your care and keeping, I give you this ring that you may place it on her finger as a token, and in pledge that you so receive her. Thus you are to compass about her life with strength and protecting love.

Then shall the minister say to the man:

_____, as a token and a pledge that you will faithfully perform your holy vows, will you receive and wear this ring?

The man shall answer:
I will.
Then the minister, addressing the woman, shall say:
_____, indicating your responsibility to
_____ to receive him into your care and devotion, I give you this ring that you may place it on his finger as a token and in pledge that you so receive him. Thus you are to encircle his life with affection and tenderness.

Addressing both the man and the woman, the minister continues:
Thus you each are to wear your ring as the enclosing bond of reverence and trust.

Thus you both are to fulfill the perfect circle of duty that makes you one.

Following the ceremony of the ring (or rings), then the minister shall say:
And now I charge upon you that love one toward another, ordained of God:
Love is patient and kind; love is not jealous or boastful; it is not arrogant or rude. Love does not insist on its own way; it is not irritable or resentful; it does not rejoice at wrong, but rejoices in the right. Love bears all things, believes all things, hopes all things, endures all things. Love never ends. . . . So faith, hope, love abide, these three; but the greatest of these is love. (I CORINTHIANS 13:4–8, 13)

Let us pray.
Then the man and the woman kneeling, the minister, and the people shall say the Lord's Prayer:
Our Father, who art in heaven, hallowed be thy name. Thy kingdom come, thy will be done on earth as it is in heaven. Give us this day our daily bread; and forgive us our debts, as we forgive our debtors; and lead us not into temptation, but deliver us from evil; for thine is the kingdom and the power and the glory forever. Amen.

Then shall the minister add:

Most merciful and gracious Father, of whom the whole family in heaven and earth is named; bestow upon these thy servants the seal of thine approval and thy fatherly benediction; granting them to fulfill, with pure and steadfast affection, the vow and covenant between them made. Guide them together, we pray, in the way of righteousness and peace, that loving and serving thee, with one heart and mind, all the days of their lives, they may be abundantly enriched with the tokens of thine everlasting favor; in Jesus Christ our Lord. Amen.

Then shall the minister join their right hands together, and say:

Those whom God has joined together let no man put asunder.

Then shall the minister, addressing the man and woman, say:

Forasmuch as you, ——————————, and you, ———————————, have covenanted together in the presence of God, and of this company, to live together in holy marriage, and have pledged the same by giving and receiving a ring, and by joining hands; I declare you to be husband and wife, in the name of the Father, and of the Son, and of the Holy Spirit.

Then the minister shall add this blessing:

The Lord bless you and keep you. The Lord make his face to shine upon you, and be gracious to you. The Lord lift up his countenance upon you and give you peace. Amen.

The minister may add this benediction:

And now may he who walked in intimate companionship with the first human pair in the days of their innocence; and he who coming in sorrow made the marriage feast to rejoice by his miraculous ministry; and he who dwelling in your hearts can make your house a habitation of love and peace —the Father, Son, and Holy Spirit—be with you evermore. Amen.

A COMMUNITY OR CONGREGATIONAL MARRIAGE SERVICE[3]

(Used by Dr. Roy A. Burkhart)

Coming as they do to dedicate themselves unto God, and with His eternal help to fashion their house into a home, the hearth into an altar, their family into a unit of His kingdom; and to achieve within their love the very hint of eternity, ——————— and ——————— come seeking the sacrament of holy marriage.

Let us pray: O Thou infinite Father, bless these who come here in this high moment of their lives together. We thank Thee for all of the rich values which have flowed into them from those who loved them and nurtured them and pointed them to the way of life. We thank Thee that Thou has hidden within them the dream of a great love, and that now Thou wilt help them fashion it into a home that shall endure. We thank Thee for the values they have found by their own striving. And now as they make their promises to each other, may they make them with the deepest insight into their meaning and with their fullest sincerity. And do grant unto them the gift of a great love, and the vision of the strength to build it with Christ as the living presence, into a home that will glorify Him, for in His name we pray. Amen.

I charge you both, as you stand in the presence of God, to remember that love and loyalty alone will avail as the foundations of a happy and enduring home. If the solemn vows which you are about to make be kept permanent, and if steadfastly you seek to do the will of your Heavenly Father, your life will be full of peace and joy, and the home which you are establishing will abide through every change.

I charge you both to grow to that place where each gets major satisfaction from giving peace and happiness to the other.

If you desire this new estate to be permanent, then cherish the vision of your first love. . . . Let it not be tarnished by the common events. Believe in this ideal you both share; it is binding; it is inviolate and in all human relations it is the final truth.

And I charge you further, by God's grace, ever to be true to the words of one who said:

> "How do I love thee? Let me count the ways.
> I love thee to the depth and breadth and height
> My soul can reach. . . .
>
> .   .   .   .
>
> I love thee to the level of everyday's
> Most quiet need, by sun and candle-light.
> I love thee freely, as men strive for Right;
> I love thee purely, as they turn from Praise.
>
> .   .   .   .
>
> . . . I love thee with the breath,
> Smiles, tears, of all my life!—and, if God choose,
> I shall but love thee better after death."*

_____, do you take _____ to be your wedded wife, and in the presence of all these witnesses do you vow that you will do everything in your power to make your love for her a growing part of your life? Will you continue to feed it from day to day and week to week and year to year from the best resources of your living? Will you stand by her in sickness or in health, in poverty or in wealth, and will you shun all others and keep yourself to her alone so long as you both shall live?

Response:

I will.

Who gives _____ in marriage?

Do you have some vows of your love to pledge to each other?

The Groom:

I, _____, take thee, _____, to be my wedded wife, to have and to hold from this day forward, in sickness or in health, in poverty or in wealth; to love and

* Elizabeth Barrett Browning, *Sonnets from the Portuguese.*

to cherish so long as we both shall live. To this I pledge thee my faith.

The Bride:

I, _____, take thee, _____, to be my wedded husband, to have and to hold from this day forward, in sickness or in health, in poverty or in wealth; to love and to cherish so long as we both shall live. To this I pledge thee my faith.

The Groom:

With this ring I thee wed, in the name of the Father, and of the Son, and of the Holy Spirit.

The Bride:

I receive this ring as a token of my love, in the name of the Father, and of the Son, and of the Holy Spirit.

Minister:

Bless him who gives this ring and her who receives it that both may go forth with Thee as guide and ever live in Thy loving favor.

Let us kneel:

"Love through eternity endures,
    For God is Love and Love is God,
        Thank God for love—His first, then yours."

Forasmuch as _____ and _____ have consented together in holy wedlock, and have witnessed the same before God and this company and have pledged their faith and love to each other, and have declared the same by joining hands, and by the giving and receiving of a ring, I pronounce that they are husband and wife. Those whom God hath joined together, let no man put asunder. In the name of the Father, and of the Son, and of the Holy Spirit. Amen.

And now may the courage of the early morning's dawning, and the strength of the eternal hills, and the peace of the evening's ending and the love of God be in your hearts now and forevermore. Amen.

A PRESBYTERIAN MARRIAGE SERVICE[4]

The persons to be married shall present themselves before the minister, the man standing at the right hand of the woman. Then, all present reverently standing, the minister shall say:

Dearly beloved, we are assembled here in the presence of God, to join this Man and this Woman in holy marriage; which is instituted of God, regulated by His commandments, blessed by our Lord Jesus Christ, and to be held in honor among all men. Let us therefore reverently remember that God has established and sanctified marriage, for the welfare and happiness of mankind. Our Saviour has declared that a man shall leave his father and mother and cleave unto his wife. By His apostles, He has instructed those who enter into this relation to cherish a mutual esteem and love; to bear with each other's infirmities and weaknesses; to comfort each other in sickness, trouble, and sorrow; in honesty and industry to provide for each other, and for their household, in temporal things; to pray for and encourage each other in the things which pertain to God; and to live together as the heirs of the grace of life.

Forasmuch as these two Persons have come hither to be made one in this holy estate, if there be any here present who knows any just cause why they may not lawfully be joined in marriage, I require him now to make it known, or ever after to hold his peace.

Then, speaking unto the persons who are to be married, the minister shall say:

I charge you both, before the great God, the Searcher of all hearts, that if either of you know any reason why ye may not lawfully be joined together in marriage, ye do now confess it. For be ye well assured that if any persons are joined together otherwise than as God's Word allows, their union is not blessed by Him.

Then, if no impediment appear, the minister shall say:

Let us pray. Almighty and ever-blessed God, whose presence is the happiness of every condition, and whose favor hallows every relation: We beseech Thee to be present and favorable unto these Thy servants, that they may be truly joined in the honorable estate of marriage, in the covenant of their God. As Thou hast brought them together by Thy providence, sanctify them by Thy Spirit, giving them a new frame of heart fit for their new estate; and enrich them with all grace, whereby they may enjoy the comforts, undergo the cares, endure the trials, and perform the duties of life together as becometh Christians, under Thy heavenly guidance and protection; through our Lord Jesus Christ. Amen.

Then the minister, calling the man by his Christian name, shall say:

N., wilt thou have this Woman to be thy wife, and wilt thou pledge thy troth to her, in all love and honor, in all duty and service, in all faith and tenderness, to live with her, and cherish her, according to the ordinance of God, in the holy bond of marriage?

The man shall answer:

I will.

Then the minister, calling the woman by her Christian name, shall say:

N., wilt thou have this Man to be thy husband, and wilt thou pledge thy troth to him, in all love and honor, in all duty and service, in all faith and tenderness, to live with him, and cherish him, according to the ordinance of God, in the holy bond of marriage?

The woman shall answer:

I will.

Then the minister may say:

Who giveth this Woman to be married to this Man?

Then the father, or guardian, or friend, of the woman shall put her right hand in the hand of the minister, who shall cause the man with his right hand to take the woman by her right hand and to say after the minister, as follows:

I, N., take thee, N., to be my wedded wife; and I do promise and covenant, before God and these witnesses, to be thy loving and faithful husband, in plenty and in want, in joy and in sorrow, in sickness and in health, as long as we both shall live.

Then shall they loose their hands; and the woman, with her right hand taking the man by his right hand, shall likewise say after the minister:

I, N., take thee, N., to be my wedded husband; and I do promise and covenant, before God and these witnesses, to be thy loving and faithful wife, in plenty and in want, in joy and in sorrow, in sickness and in health, as long as we both shall live.

Then, if a ring be provided, it shall be given to the minister, who shall return it to the man, who shall then put it upon the fourth finger of the woman's left hand, saying after the minister:

This ring I give thee in token and pledge of our constant faith and abiding love.

Or:

With this ring I thee wed, in the name of the Father, and of the Son, and of the Holy Spirit. Amen.

Before giving the ring, the minister may say:

Bless, O Lord, this ring, that he who gives it and she who wears it may abide in Thy peace, and continue in Thy favor, unto their life's end; through Jesus Christ our Lord. Amen.

If a second ring be provided, a similar order shall be followed, the woman saying the same words after the minister.

Then the minister shall say:

Let us pray. Most merciful and gracious God, of whom the whole family in heaven and earth is named: Bestow upon these Thy servants the seal of Thine approval, and Thy Fatherly benediction; granting unto them grace to fulfill, with pure and steadfast affection, the vow and covenant between them made. Guide them together, we beseech Thee, in the way of righteousness and peace, that, loving and serving Thee, with one heart and mind, all the days of their life, they may be abundantly enriched with the tokens of Thine everlasting favor, in Jesus Christ our Lord. Amen.

Then the minister and people shall say:

Our Father, who art in heaven, hallowed be Thy name. Thy kingdom come, Thy will be done on earth as it is in heaven. Give us this day our daily bread; and forgive us our debts, as we forgive our debtors; and lead us not into temptation, but deliver us from evil; for Thine is the kingdom, and the power, and the glory forever. Amen.

Then shall the minister say unto all who are present:

By the authority committed unto me as a Minister of the Church of Christ, I declare that N. and N. are now Husband and Wife, according to the ordinance of God, and the law of the State, in the name of the Father, and of the Son, and of the Holy Spirit. Amen.

Then, causing the husband and wife to join their right hands, the minister shall say:

Whom therefore God hath joined together, let no man put asunder.

It is fitting that the bride and groom kneel to receive the benediction:

The Lord bless you and keep you. The Lord make His face to shine upon you and be gracious unto you. The Lord lift up His countenance upon you and give you peace, both now and in the life everlasting. Amen.

Or:

God the Father, God the Son, God the Holy Spirit, bless, preserve, and keep you; the Lord mercifully with His favor look upon you, and fill you with all spiritual benediction and grace; that ye may so live together in this life, that in the world to come ye may have life everlasting. Amen.

A METHODIST MARRIAGE SERVICE[5]

Dearly beloved, we are gathered together here in the sight of God, and in the presence of these witnesses, to join together this man and this woman in holy matrimony;

which is an honorable estate, instituted of God, and signifying unto us the mystical union which exists between Christ and his Church; which holy estate Christ adorned and beautified with his presence in Cana of Galilee. It is therefore not to be entered into unadvisedly, but reverently, discreetly, and in the fear of God. Into this holy estate these two persons come now to be joined. If any man can show just cause why they may not lawfully be joined together, let him now speak, or else hereafter forever hold his peace.

Addressing the persons to be married, the minister shall say:

I require and charge you both, as you stand in the presence of God, before whom the secrets of all hearts are disclosed, that having duly considered the holy covenant you are about to make, you do now declare before this company your pledge of faith, each to the other. Be well assured that if these solemn vows are kept inviolate, as God's Word demands, and if steadfastly you endeavor to do the will of your heavenly Father, God will bless your marriage, will grant you fulfillment in it, and will establish your home in peace.

Then shall the minister say to the man, using his Christian name:

N., wilt thou have this woman to be thy wedded wife, to live together in the holy estate of matrimony? Wilt thou love her, comfort her, honor and keep her, in sickness and in health; and forsaking all other keep thee only unto her so long as ye both shall live?

The man shall answer:

I will.

Then shall the minister say to the woman, using her Christian name:

N., wilt thou have this man to be thy wedded husband, to live together in the holy estate of matrimony? Wilt thou love him, comfort him, honor and keep him, in sickness and in health; and forsaking all others keep thee only unto him so long as ye both shall live?

The woman shall answer:
I will.
Then shall the minister say:
Who giveth this woman to be married to this man?
The father of the woman, or whoever gives her in marriage, shall answer:
I do.
Then the minister, receiving the hand of the woman from her father or other sponsor, shall cause the man with his right hand to take the woman by her right hand, and say after him:

I, N., take thee, N., to be my wedded wife, to have and to hold, from this day forward, for better for worse, for richer for poorer, in sickness and in health, to love and to cherish, till death us do part, according to God's holy ordinance; and thereto I pledge thee my faith.

Then shall they loose their hands; and the woman, with her right hand taking the man by his right hand, shall say after the minister:

I, N., take thee, N., to be my wedded husband, to have and to hold, from this day forward, for better for worse, for richer for poorer, in sickness and in health, to love and to cherish, till death us do part, according to God's holy ordinance; and thereto I pledge thee my faith.

Then they may give to each other rings, or the man may give to the woman a ring, in this wise: the minister taking the ring or rings, shall say:

The wedding ring is the outward and visible sign of an inward and spiritual grace, signifying to all the uniting of this man and this woman in holy matrimony, through the Church of Jesus Christ our Lord.

Then the minister may say:
Let us pray. Bless, O Lord, the giving of these rings, that they who wear them may abide in thy peace, and continue in thy favor; through Jesus Christ our Lord. Amen.

Or, if there be but one ring, the minister may say:
Bless, O Lord, the giving of this ring, that he who gives

it and she who wears it may abide forever in thy peace, and continue in thy favor; through Jesus Christ our Lord. Amen.

The minister shall then deliver the proper ring to the man to put upon the third finger of the woman's left hand. The man, holding the ring there, shall say after the minister:

In token and pledge of our constant faith and abiding love, with this ring I thee wed, in the name of the Father, and of the Son, and of the Holy Spirit. Amen.

Then, if there is a second ring, the minister shall deliver it to the woman to put upon the third finger of the man's left hand; and the woman, holding the ring there, shall say after the minister:

In token and pledge of our constant faith and abiding love, with this ring I thee wed, in the name of the Father, and of the Son, and of the Holy Spirit. Amen.

Then shall the minister join their right hands together and, with his hand on their united hands, shall say:

Forasmuch as N. and N. have consented together in holy wedlock, and have witnessed the same before God and this company, and thereto have pledged their faith each to the other and have declared the same by joining hands and by giving and receiving rings; I pronounce that they are husband and wife together, in the name of the Father, and of the Son, and of the Holy Spirit. Those whom God hath joined together, let not man put asunder. Amen.

Then shall the minister say:

Let us pray.

Then shall the husband and wife kneel; the minister shall say:

O eternal God, creator and preserver of all mankind, giver of all spiritual grace, the author of everlasting life: Send thy blessing upon this man and this woman, whom we bless in thy name; that they may surely perform and keep the vow and covenant between them made, and may ever remain in perfect love and peace together, and live according to thy laws.

Look graciously upon them, that they may love, honor, and cherish each other, and so live together in faithfulness and patience, in wisdom and true godliness, that their home may be a haven of blessing and a place of peace; through Jesus Christ our Lord. Amen.

Then the husband and wife, still kneeling, shall join with the minister and congregation in the lord's prayer, saying:

Our Father, who art in heaven, hallowed be thy name. Thy kingdom come, thy will be done on earth as it is in heaven. Give us this day our daily bread; and forgive us our trespasses, as we forgive those who trespass against us; and lead us not into temptation, but deliver us from evil; for thine is the kingdom, and the power, and the glory forever. Amen.

Then the minister shall give this blessing:

God the Father, the Son, and the Holy Spirit bless, preserve, and keep you; the Lord graciously with his favor look upon you, and so fill you with all spiritual benediction and love that you may so live together in this life that in the world to come you may have life everlasting. Amen.

A LUTHERAN MARRIAGE SERVICE[6]

The persons to be married, having presented themselves at the entrance to the chancel, the man to the right of the woman, a suitable hymn may be sung.

The minister shall say or chant:

In the name of the Father and of the Son and of the Holy Ghost.

The congregation shall say or chant:

Amen.

The minister shall read a suitable scripture lesson, such as John 2:1–11 or Psalm 67 or Psalm 23. If the minister reads a Psalm, the congregation shall respond by singing the Gloria Patri.

The minister, standing before the bridal pair, at the entrance to the chancel, may give the address. Then the minister shall say:

Dearly Beloved: Whereas you desire to enter upon the holy estate of matrimony, ordained of God, and to be held in honor by all, it becometh you, with reverent minds, to hear what the Word of God teacheth concerning this estate:

The Lord God saith, "It is not good that the man should be alone; I will make him an help meet for him."

Our Lord Jesus Christ saith: "Have ye not read that He which made them at the beginning, made them male and female, and said, 'For this cause shall a man leave father and mother and shall cleave to his wife; and they twain shall be one flesh'? Wherefore they are no more twain, but one flesh. What therefore God hath joined together, let not man put asunder."

The Apostle Paul, speaking by the Holy Ghost, saith: "Husbands, love your wives, even as Christ also loved the Church, and gave Himself for it. So ought men to love their wives as their own bodies. He that loveth his wife loveth himself. For no man ever yet hated his own flesh, but nourisheth and cherisheth it, even as the Lord the Church. Wives, submit yourselves unto your own husbands as unto the Lord. For the husband is the head of the wife, even as Christ is the Head of the Church; and He is the Saviour of the body. Therefore as the Church is subject unto Christ, so let the wives be to their own husbands in everything."

And although, by reason of sin, many a cross hath been laid upon this estate, nevertheless our gracious Father in heaven doth not forsake His children in an estate so holy and acceptable to Him, but is ever present with His bountiful blessings.

For thus saith the Lord in the Psalm: "Blessed is everyone that feareth the Lord, that walketh in His ways. For thou shalt eat the labor of thine hands. Happy shalt thou be, and it shall be well with thee. Thy wife shall be as a fruitful vine by the sides of thine house; thy children like olive plants round about thy table. Behold, that thus shall the man be blessed that feareth the Lord. The Lord shall bless thee out of Zion; and thou shalt see the good of Jerusalem all the days of thy life. Yea, thou shalt see thy children's children and peace upon Israel."

Thus hath our heavenly Father sanctified the estate of matrimony. He will ever bless therein all who love Him, trust in Him, and live in His fear, for Jesus' sake.

Dearly beloved, you have come here to be united into this holy estate, which consisteth in your mutual consent, sincerely and freely given; it behooveth you, then, to declare, in the presence of God and these witnesses, the sincere intent you both have.

Then the minister may say:

Who giveth this woman to be married to this man?

The father or another relative shall say:

I do.

Then shall the minister say to the man:

N., wilt thou have this woman to be thy wedded wife, to live with her after God's ordinance in the holy estate of matrimony? Wilt thou love her, comfort her, honor her, and keep her in sickness and in health, and, forsaking all others, keep thee only unto her, so long as ye both shall live?

The man shall say:

I will.

Then shall the minister say to the woman:

N., wilt thou have this man to be thy wedded husband, to live with him after God's ordinance in the holy estate of matrimony? Wilt thou love him, comfort him, honor him, obey him, and keep him in sickness and in health, and, forsaking all others, keep thee only unto him, so long as ye both shall live?

The woman shall say:

I will.

Then may the minister place the right hand of the woman in the right hand of the man. Then shall they loose their hands.

Then shall the minister precede the man and the woman

to the altar. The veil of the woman shall be lifted. The man, facing the woman, shall take the right hand of the woman, facing him, and say after the minister:

I, N., in the presence of God and these witnesses, take thee, N., to be my wedded wife, and plight thee my troth, till death us do part.

Then shall the woman, in like manner, say after the minister:

I, N., in the presence of God and these witnesses, take thee, N., to be my wedded husband, and plight thee my troth, till death us do part.

If the wedding ring be used, the minister shall now receive it and deliver it to the man, to be put on the fourth finger of the woman's left hand.

Then shall the man say, or, if two rings be used, the man and the woman, in turn, shall say, after the minister:

Receive this ring as a pledge and token of wedded love and faithfulness.

Then shall the minister say:

May the giving and receiving of this ring (these rings) ever be a symbol of the faithful and unselfish community of goods that you as husband and wife, in weal and woe, will cultivate without ceasing, and be a reminder of the excellent Christian virtues with which you will adorn your marriage. To this end may God bless you through the heavenly Bridegroom, Jesus Christ, our Lord.

Then shall the minister say:

Join your right hands.

Then shall the minister lay his right hand upon their hands and say:

Forasmuch as N. and N. have consented together in holy wedlock and have declared the same before God and these witnesses, I pronounce them husband and wife, in the name of the Father and of the Son and of the Holy Ghost. Amen.

What therefore God hath joined together, let not man put asunder.

Then shall they turn to face the altar and kneel, and the minister shall bless them, saying:

May the Almighty and Eternal God look down from His exalted throne in heaven upon you with His favor, and sanctify and bless you with the benediction first spoken to Adam and Eve in Paradise, that you may please Him both in body and soul, and live together in holy love until life's end.

The eternal God, the Father of our Lord Jesus Christ, bestow upon you His Holy Spirit and be with you and richly bless you forevermore. Amen.

Or:

The God of Abraham, the God of Isaac, the God of Jacob, be with you and richly bless you forevermore. Amen.

Then shall the man and the woman rise and stand facing the altar. If no hymn is sung, they remain kneeling.

Then may a suitable hymn be sung.

Then shall the man and the woman kneel.

Then shall the minister say or chant:

Let us pray: Almighty, eternal God, our heavenly Father, who hast united this man and this woman in the holy estate of matrimony, grant them the grace to live therein according to Thy Word; strengthen them in constant faithfulness and true love toward each other; sustain and defend them amidst all trials and temptations; and help them so to pass through this world in faith towards Thee, in communion with Thy holy Church, and in loving service one of the other, that they may ever enjoy Thy heavenly benediction; through Jesus Christ, Thy Son, our Lord, who liveth and reigneth with Thee and the Holy Ghost, ever one God, world without end.

The congregation shall say or chant:

Amen.

Then shall all say:

Our Father, who art in heaven, hallowed be Thy name. Thy kingdom come, Thy will be done on earth as it is in heaven. Give us this day our daily bread; and forgive us our trespasses, as we forgive those who trespass against us; and lead us not into temptation, but deliver us from evil; for Thine is the kingdom and the power and the glory forever and ever. Amen.

Then shall the minister say or chant the benediction:

The Lord bless thee and keep thee. The Lord make His face shine upon thee and be gracious unto thee. The Lord lift up His countenance upon thee and give thee peace.

Then shall the congregation say or chant:

Amen.

Silent prayer.

THE EPISCOPAL MARRIAGE SERVICE[7]

At the day and time appointed for solemnization of matrimony, the persons to be married shall come into the body of the church, or shall be ready in some proper house, with their friends and neighbors; and there standing together, the man on the right hand, and the woman on the left, the minister shall say:

Dearly beloved, we are gathered together here in the sight of God, and in the face of this company, to join together this Man and this Woman in holy Matrimony; which is an honourable estate, instituted of God, signifying unto us the mystical union that is betwixt Christ and his Church: which holy estate Christ adorned and beautified with his presence and first miracle that he wrought in Cana of Galilee, and is commended of Saint Paul to be honourable among all men; and therefore is not by any to be entered into unadvisedly or lightly; but reverently, discreetly, advisedly, soberly, and in the fear of God. Into this holy estate these two persons present come now to be joined. If any man can show just cause why they may not lawfully be joined together, let him now speak, or else hereafter forever hold his peace.

And also speaking unto the persons who are to be married, he shall say:

I require and charge you both, as ye will answer at the

dreadful day of judgment when the secrets of all hearts shall be disclosed, that if either of you know any impediment, why ye may not be lawfully joined together in Matrimony, ye do now confess it. For be ye well assured, that if any persons are joined together otherwise than as God's Word doth allow, their marriage is not lawful.

The minister, if he shall have reason to doubt of the lawfulness of the proposed marriage, may demand sufficient surety for his indemnification: but if no impediment shall be alleged, or suspected, the minister shall say to the man:

_____, wilt thou have this Woman to thy wedded wife, to live together after God's ordinance in the holy estate of Matrimony? Wilt thou love her, comfort her, honour, and keep her in sickness and in health; and, forsaking all others, keep thee only unto her, so long as ye both shall live?

The man shall answer:

I will.

Then shall the minister say unto the woman:

_____, wilt thou have this Man to thy wedded husband, to live together after God's ordinance in the holy estate of Matrimony? Wilt thou love him, comfort him, honour, and keep him in sickness and in health; and, forsaking all others, keep thee only unto him, so long as ye both shall live?

The woman shall answer:

I will.

Then shall the minister say:

Who giveth this Woman to be married to this Man?

Then shall they give their troth to each other in this manner. The minister, receiving the woman at her father's or friend's hands, shall cause the man with his right hand to take the woman by her right hand, and to say after him as followeth:

I, _____, take thee, _____, to my wedded Wife, to have and to hold from this day forward, for better for worse, for richer for poorer, in sickness and in health, to love and to cherish, till death us do part, according to God's holy ordinance; and thereto I plight thee my troth.

Then shall they loose their hands; and the woman, with her right hand taking the man by his right hand, shall likewise say after the minister:

I, _____, take thee, _____, to my wedded Husband, to have and to hold from this day forward, for better for worse, for richer for poorer, in sickness and in health, to love and to cherish, till death us do part, according to God's holy ordinance; and thereto I give thee my troth.

Then shall they again loose their hands; and the man shall give unto the woman a ring in this wise: the minister, taking the ring, shall deliver it unto the man, to put it upon the fourth finger of the woman's left hand. And the man, holding the ring there, and taught by the minister, shall say:

With this ring I thee wed, in the Name of the Father, and of the Son, and of the Holy Ghost. Amen.

And, before delivering the ring to the man, the minister may say as followeth:

Bless, O Lord, this ring, that he who gives it and she who wears it may abide in thy peace, and continue in thy favour, unto their life's end; through Jesus Christ our Lord. Amen.

Then, the man leaving the ring upon the fourth finger of the woman's left hand, the minister shall say:

Let us pray.

Then shall the minister and the people, still standing, say the Lord's Prayer:

Our Father, who art in heaven, hallowed be Thy name. Thy kingdom come, thy will be done on earth as it is in heaven. Give us this day our daily bread; and forgive us our trespasses, as we forgive those who trespass against us; and lead us not into temptation, but deliver us from evil; for thine is the kingdom, and the power, and the glory, for ever and ever. Amen.

Then shall the minister add:

O eternal God, Creator and Preserver of all mankind, Giver of all spiritual grace, the Author of everlasting life; send thy blessing upon these thy servants, this man and this woman, whom we bless in thy Name; that they, living faithfully together, may surely perform and keep the vow and covenant betwixt them made (whereof this ring given and received is a token and pledge), and may ever remain in perfect love and peace together, and live according to thy laws; through Jesus Christ our Lord. Amen.

The minister may add one or both of the following prayers:

O Almighty God, Creator of mankind, who only art the well-spring of life; bestow upon these thy servants, if it be thy will, the gift and heritage of children; and grant that they may see their children brought up in thy faith and fear, to the honour and glory of thy Name; through Jesus Christ our Lord. Amen.

O God, who hast so consecrated the state of Matrimony that in it is represented the spiritual marriage and unity betwixt Christ and his Church; look mercifully upon these thy servants, that they may love, honour, and cherish each other, and so live together in faithfulness and patience, in wisdom and true godliness, that their home may be a haven of blessing and of peace; through the same Jesus Christ our Lord, who liveth and reigneth with thee and the Holy Spirit ever, one God, world without end. Amen.

Then shall the minister join their right hands together, and say:

Those whom God hath joined together let no man put asunder.

Then shall the minister speak unto the company:

Forasmuch as _____ and _____ have consented together in holy wedlock, and have witnessed the same before God and this company, and thereto have given and pledged their troth, each to the other, and have declared the same by giving and receiving a ring, and by joining hands; I pronounce that they are Man and Wife, in the Name of the Father, and of the Son, and of the Holy Ghost. Amen.

The man and wife kneeling, the minister shall add this blessing:

God the Father, God the Son, God the Holy Ghost, bless, preserve, and keep you; the Lord mercifully with his favour look upon you, and fill you with all spiritual benediction and grace; that ye may so live together in this life, that in the world to come ye may have life everlasting. Amen.

A GENERAL MARRIAGE SERVICE[8]

(Where a wedding is to be performed at home and it is desired to be done with dignified simplicity, the following form may be employed.)

The persons to be married standing, facing the minister. He shall first address the company, and shall say:

Dearly beloved, we are gathered together here in the presence of God and in the face of this company, to join together this man and this woman in Holy Matrimony; which is an honorable estate, instituted of God in the time of man's innocency, and adorned by our Lord Jesus Christ by his presence and the first miracle that he wrought in Cana of Galilee, and is commended by the Apostle Paul to be honorable among all men; and therefore is not by any to be entered upon lightly and unadvisedly, but reverently, soberly, discreetly and in the fear of God. Into this goodly estate these two persons present come now to be joined; and we are here to wish them joy as they go forth to the establishment of a new home.

Then shall the minister, calling him by his first name, address the man, saying:

_____, wilt thou have this woman to thy wedded wife, to live together after God's own ordinance in the holy estate of matrimony? Wilt thou love her, cherish her, honor her and protect her in sickness and in health, and forsaking all others keep thee only unto her so long as you both shall live?

The man shall answer:

I will.

Then shall the minister say to the woman:

_____, wilt thou have this man to thy wedded husband, to live together after God's own ordinance in the holy estate of matrimony? Wilt thou love him, honor him, cherish and comfort him in sickness and in health, and forsaking all others keep thee only unto him so long as you both shall live?

The woman shall answer:

I will.

When it is desired that the bride be given away, the minister shall ask:

Who giveth this woman to be married to this man?

The minister, receiving the woman at her father's or friend's hands, shall cause the man with his right hand to take the woman by her right hand and say after him, as follows:

I, _____, take thee, _____, to my wedded wife, to have and to hold from this day forward, for better for worse, for richer for poorer, in sickness and in health, to love and to cherish, until death us do part, according to God's holy ordinance, and therefore I plight thee my troth.

While they still hold each other's hands, the woman shall say after the minister:

I, _____, take thee, _____, to my wedded husband, to have and to hold, from this day forward, for better for worse, for richer for poorer, in sickness and in health, to love and to cherish, until death us do part, according to God's holy ordinance, and thereto I give thee my troth.

Then may the man produce a ring and hand it to the minister, and the minister, taking the ring, shall deliver it to the man to put upon the fourth finger of the woman's left hand, and the man, during the act of placing the ring, shall say after the minister:

With this ring I thee wed, and with all my worldly goods I thee endow, in the name of the Father, and of the Son, and of the Holy Ghost. Amen.

Then shall the minister speak unto the company:

For as much as _____ and _____ have promised to be faithful and true each to the other, and have witnessed the same before God and this company by giving and receiving a ring and by joining hands, now therefore, in accordance with the laws of God and the State of _____, I pronounce them husband and wife. Those whom God hath joined together, let no man put asunder. Let us pray.

Then shall they kneel, and the minister shall offer prayer, and the prayer may conclude with the following blessing:

The Lord God almighty, bless, preserve and keep you. The Lord with his favor mercifully look upon you and fill you with all spiritual benediction and grace that you may so live together in this life that in the world to come you may have life everlasting, through Jesus Christ, our Lord. Amen.

ORDER FOR BLESSING OF A CIVIL MARRIAGE[9]

The minister, satisfied that the persons seeking this blessing have been lawfully married, shall say:

Dearly beloved, we are met here in the presence of God to invoke the blessings of the Heavenly Father upon your marriage. Let us reverently bring to remembrance that marriage was instituted by God for the comfort and help of his children and that families might be trained in goodness and godliness of life. Both by his presence and his solemn words, Christ honored and sanctioned it; and it is set forth and commended in the Scripture as honorable to all who enter it lawfully, seriously, and with true affection.

The minister then, asking the man to take the right hand of the woman in his right hand, shall say:

_____, do you before God and these witnesses acknowledge this woman to be your lawful wedded wife; and do you promise that from this day forward you will be her faithful husband, for better for worse, for richer for poorer, in sickness and in health, to love and to cherish, till death do you part?

The man shall answer:

I do.

The minister then, asking the woman to take the right hand of the man in her right hand, shall say:

_____, do you before God and these witnesses acknowledge this man to be your lawful wedded husband; and do you promise that from this day forward you will be his faithful wife, for better for worse, for richer for poorer, in sickness and in health, to love and to cherish, till death do you part?

The woman shall answer:

I do.

If a ring be provided, the minister, upon receiving it, shall give it to the man, requesting him, as he places it upon the fourth finger of the woman's left hand, to say:

In pledge of the vow made between us, I give thee this ring; in the name of the Father, and of the Son, and of the Holy Spirit. Amen.

Then the minister shall say:

Let us pray. O eternal God, Creator and Preserver of all mankind, Giver of all spiritual grace, the Author of everlasting life: Send thy blessing upon these thy servants, this man and this woman, whom we bless in thy Name; that they, living faithfully together, may surely perform and keep the vow and covenant betwixt them made, and may ever remain in perfect love and peace together, and live according to thy laws, through Jesus Christ our Lord. Amen.

Then the minister and people shall say:

Our Father, who art in heaven, hallowed be thy name. Thy kingdom come, thy will be done on earth as it is in heaven. Give us this day our daily bread; and forgive us our debts, as we forgive our debtors; and lead us not into temptation, but deliver us from evil; for thine is the kingdom, and the power, and the glory, forever. Amen.

The bride and groom, kneeling to receive the benediction, the minister shall say:

God the Father, God the Son, God the Holy Spirit, bless, preserve, and keep you; the Lord mercifully with his favor look upon you, and fill you with all spiritual benediction and grace; that you may so live together in this life, that in the world to come you may have life everlasting. Amen.

Sources, Further Reading, Bibliography

PREFACE
1. Hedley, George, *Christian Worship* (New York, Macmillan Co., 1953) pp. 209–10.

CHAPTER I

Sources
1. Trueblood, Elton and Pauline, *The Recovery of Family Life* (New York, Harper & Row Publishers, Inc., 1953) p. 40.
2. Pearson, Ray, "No Longer Two," *Pulpit Digest* (June 1958) pp. 27–33.

Further Reading
1. Bowman, Henry A., *A Christian Interpretation of Marriage* (Philadelphia, Westminster Press, 1959).
2. Daves, Michael, "Making the Wedding Service Christian," *Pulpit Digest* (Jan. 1965) pp. 19–22.
3. Hedley, George, *Christian Worship* (New York, Macmillan Company, 1953).
4. Mace, David R., *Whom God Hath Joined* (Philadelphia, Westminster Press, 1953).
5. Ray, Randolph, *Marriage is Serious Business* (New York, Whittlesey House, McGraw-Hill Book Company, 1944).

CHAPTER II

Sources
1. Belting, Natalia, and Hine, James R., *Your Wedding Workbook* (Danville, Ill., Interstate Printers & Publishers, Inc., 1963) pp. 3, 4.

2. Central Christian Church, Enid, Oklahoma.
3. Hine, James R., *Grounds for Marriage* (Danvil'e, Ill., Interstate Printers & Publishers, Inc., 1962) pp. 75–7.

Further Reading

1. Belting, Natalia, and Hine, James R., *Your Wedding Workbook* (Danville, Ill., Interstate Printers & Publishers, Inc., 1963).
2. Bentley, Marguerite Logan, *Wedding Etiquette Complete* (Philadelphia, Holt, Rinehart & Winston, Inc., 1956).
3. Newton, Sallie, *How to Plan a Beautiful Wedding* (Houston, Texas, 1954).
4. Post, Emily, *Etiquette: The Blue Book of Social Usage,* 11th edition (New York, Funk & Wagnalls Company, 1965).
5. Taylor, Jabez, *Wedding Etiquette* (Grand Rapids, Mich., Zondervan Publishing House, 1946).
6. Vanderbilt, Amy, *New Complete Book of Etiquette* (Garden City, N. Y., Doubleday & Company, Inc., 1963).

CHAPTER III

Sources

1. Daves, Michael, "Making the Wedding Service Christian," *Pulpit Digest* (Jan. 1965) pp. 19–22.

Further Reading

1. Hedley, George, *Christian Worship* (New York, Macmillan Company, 1953).
2. Lovelace, Austin C., and Rice, William C., *Music and Worship in the Church* (Nashville, Tenn., Abingdon Press, 1960).
3. Squire, Russel N., *Church Music* (St. Louis, Mo., Bethany Press, 1962).

CHAPTER IV

Sources

1. Desmond, George C., "A Program of Premarital Counseling," *Pulpit Digest* (Oct. 1963) pp. 17–21.
2. Butterfield, Oliver M., in *Pre-Marital Counseling: A Manual*

of Suggestions for Ministers (New York, Commission on Marriage and Home, Federal Council of Churches of Christ in America, 1945) pp. 31, 32.
3. Hine, James R., *Grounds for Marriage* (Danville, Ill., Interstate Printers & Publishers, Inc., 1962) pp. vii, viii; 75–7.

Further Reading

1. Abraham, Stan, and Levine, Leana, *The Pre-Marital Consultation* (New York, Grune and Stratton, Inc., 1956).
2. Adams, Clifford R., *Preparing for Marriage* (New York, E. P. Dutton & Company, 1951).
3. Bowman, Henry A., *A Christian Interpretation of Marriage* (Philadelphia, Westminster Press, 1959).
4. Butterfield, Oliver M., *Planning for Marriage* (Princeton, N. J., D. Van Nostrand Co., Inc., 1956).
5. Butterfield, Oliver M., *Sexual Harmony in Marriage* (New York, Emerson Books, Inc., 1962) revised ed.
6. Dicks, Russell L., *Premarital Guidance* (Englewood Cliffs, N. J., Prentice-Hall, Inc., 1963).
7. Duvall, Evelyn M., and Hill, Reuben L., *When You Marry* (New York, Association Press, 1945).
8. Duvall, Sylvanus, M., *Before You Marry* (New York, Association Press, 1959).
9. Hine, James R., *Grounds for Marriage* (Danville, Ill., Interstate Printers & Publishers, Inc., 1962).
10. Linn, Louis, and Schwarz, Leo W., *Psychiatry and Religious Experience* (New York, Random House, Inc., 1958).
11. Morris, J. Kenneth, *Premarital Counseling: A Manual for Ministers* (Englewood Cliffs, N. J., Prentice-Hall, Inc., 1960).
12. Mudd, Emily H., *The Practise of Marriage Counseling* (New York, Association Press, 1951).
13. Mudd, Emily H., and others (editors), *Marriage Counseling: A Casebook* (New York, Association Press, 1958).
14. Oates, Wayne E., *Premarital Counseling Care and Counseling* (Nashville, Tenn., Broadman Press, 1958).
15. Pike, James A., *If You Marry Outside Your Faith* (New York, Harper & Row Publishers, Inc., 1954).
16. Piper, Otto A., *A Biblical View of Sex and Marriage* (New York, Charles Scribner's Sons, 1960).

17. *Premarital Counseling Booklet,* (Federal Council of Churches of Christ, New York, 1945).

18. Skidmore, Rex A., Garrett, Hulda Van Streeter, Skidmore, C. Jay, *Marriage Consulting* (New York, Harper & Row Publishers, Inc., 1956).

19. Westberg, Granger, *Premarital Counseling* (New York, National Council of Churches, 1958).

20. Wynn, John Charles, *Pastoral Ministry to Families* (Philadelphia, Westminster Press, 1957).

Bibliography of written materials that may be placed in hands of counselees

Appelhof, Gilbert, Jr., *You Can Be Happily Married* (New York, Macmillan Company, 1941).

Arden, Theodore Z., *Handbook for Husbands and Wives* (New York, Association Press).

Belting, Natalie, and Hine, James R., *Your Wedding Workbook* (Danville, Ill., Interstate Printers & Publishers, Inc., 1963).

Bowman, Henry A., *Marriage for Moderns* (New York, Mc-Graw-Hill Book Company, Inc., 1960).

Brink, Frederick W., *This Man and This Woman* (New York, Association Press, 1948).

Burkhart, Roy A., *A Guide for a Man and Woman Looking Toward Marriage* (Flushing, N. Y., Hearthside Press, Inc., 1943).

Butterfield, Oliver M., *Sexual Harmony in Marriage* (New York, Emerson Books, Inc., 1962) revised ed.

Fishbein, Morris, and Burgess, Ernest W. (editors), *Successful Marriage* (Garden City, N. Y., Doubleday & Company, Inc., 1955).

Henry, Joseph B., *Fulfillment in Marriage* (Westwood, N. J., Fleming H. Revell, 1966).

Hine, James R., *Grounds for Marriage* (Danville, Ill., Interstate Printers & Publishers, Inc., 1963).

Johnson, Randolf, and Pixley, *Looking Toward Marriage*

Landis, Judson T. and Mary G., *The Marriage Handbook*

Lasser, Jacob K., and Porter, Sylvia F., *Managing Your Money* (New York, Holt, Rinehart & Winston, Inc., 1953).

The Marriage Counseling Kit (cards), (Danville, Ill., Interstate Printers & Publishers, Inc., 1963).

Lewin and Gilmore, *Sex Without Fear* (Medical Research Press).

Overton, Grace Sloan, *In Love, Marriage, and Parenthood* (New York, Harper & Row Publishers, Inc.).

Peterson, James A., *Education for Marriage* (New York, Charles Scribner's Sons, 1956).

Popenoe, Paul, *Preparation for Marriage* (Los Angeles, Institute of Family Relationships).

Ray, Randolph, *Marriage Is Serious Business* (New York, Whittlesey House, 1944).

Taylor, Jabez, *Wedding Etiquette* (Grand Rapids, Mich., Zondervan Publishing House, 1946).

Wood, Leland Foster, and Dickinson, R. L., *Harmony in Marriage* (Manhasset, N. Y., Round Table Press, 1960).

CHAPTER V

Further Reading

1. Benton, Frances, *Etiquette* (New York, Random House, Inc., 1956).
2. Post, Emily, *Etiquette: The Blue Book of Social Usage* (New York, Funk & Wagnalls Company, 1965).
3. Vanderbilt, Amy, *New Complete Book of Etiquette* (Garden City, N. Y., Doubleday & Company, Inc., 1963).

CHAPTER VI

Sources

1. Vanderbilt, Amy, *New Complete Book of Etiquette* (Garden City, N. Y., Doubleday & Company, Inc., 1963) p. 84.

Further Reading

Same as Sources and Further Reading for Chapter II

CHAPTER VII

Sources

1. *The 1966 World Almanac and Book of Facts* (New York, New York World Telegram) p. 301; Mariano, William E.

(compiler), information on grounds for divorce and marriage, Council on Marriage Relations, Inc., N. Y.
2. Golenpaul, Dan (editor), and Associates, *Information Please Almanac, Atlas and Yearbook* (New York, Simon and Schuster Publishers).
3. Kupferman, Theodore R. (editor), *The Family Legal Advisor* (new, revised edition) (New York, Greystone Press, 1957).
4. Leach, William, *The Cokesbury Marriage Manual* (Nashville, Tenn., Abingdon Press, 1961).

Further Reading

1. Baber, Ray E., *Marriage and the Family* (New York, McGraw-Hill Book Company, Inc., 1953).
2. Bernard, Will, *Law for the Family* (New York, Charles Scribner's Sons, 1962).
3. Capitmann, William, *Everyone's Legal Adviser, A Modern Guide to the Law* (New York, Gilbert Press, distributed by Julian Messner, Inc., 1961).
4. Leach, William H. (editor), *The Cokesbury Marriage Manual* (Nashville, Tenn., Abingdon Press, 1961).
5. MacKay, Richard V., *Law of Marriage and Divorce* (Dobbs Ferry, N. Y., Oceana Publications, Inc., 1948).
6. May, Geoffrey, *Marriage Laws and Decisions in U.S.* (New York, Russell Sage Foundation, 1929).
7. Pilpel, Harriet, and Zavin, Theodora, *Your Marriage and the Law* (New York, Holt, Rinehart & Winston, 1952).
8. Richardson, Mary Ellen, *Marriage and the State* (New York, Russell Sage Foundation, 1929).

CHAPTER VIII

Sources

1. From "A Wedding at Countryside Christian Church," Mission, Kansas (not copyrighted).
2. Strait, C. Neil (Church of the Nazarene, Carmi, Ill.) prayer, *Pulpit Digest* (June 1964) p. 46.
3. Hayward, Percy Roy, *Young People's Prayers* (New York, Association Press, 1945) p. 62.

4. Burkhart, Roy A., *Secret of a Happy Marriage* (New York, Harper & Row Publishers, Inc., 1949) p. 63.
5. Bushnell, Horace, in *Manual of Forms for Ministers* by Benjamin L. Smith (St. Louis, Mo., Christian Board of Publication, 1919) p. 22.

CHAPTER IX

Sources

1. Hobbs, James Randolph, *Pastor's Manual* (Nashville, Tenn., Broadman Press, 1955) pp. 151–6.
2. Osborn, G. Edwin (editor), *Christian Worship—A Service Book* (St. Louis, Mo., Christian Board of Publication, 1953) pp. 67–72.
3. Burkhart, Roy A., *Secret of a Happy Marriage* (New York, Harper & Row Publishers, Inc., 1949) pp. 60–3.
4. *The Book of Common Worship,* Board of Christian Education of the Presbyterian Church in the U.S.A., approved by the General Assembly of the United Presbyterian Church, U.S.A., 1946, pp. 183–8.
5. *Ritual, The Methodist Church* (Nashville, Tenn., Board of Publication of The Methodist Church, Inc., 1964) p. 33.
6. *The Pastor's Companion* (St. Louis, Mo., Concordia Publishing House) pp. 35–41.
7. *The Book of Common Prayer of the Episcopal Church* (1549) pp. 300–4.
8. Smith, Benjamin L., *Manual of Forms for Ministers* (St. Louis, Mo., Christian Board of Publication, 1919) pp. 17–19.
9. *A Book of Worship for Free Churches* (New York, Oxford University Press, Inc., 1948) pp. 157–9. Copyright 1948 by the Board of Home Missions of the Congregational and Christian Churches; all rights reserved.